AM I DEPRESSED
Or Am I Bipolar?

© MICHAEL R. BINDER, M.D.
August 19th, 2009

Note: This book was written for educational purposes and to help patients better communicate their symptoms to their health care providers. It is not intended to be used for self-diagnoses or treatment. Anyone suspected of having a psychiatric condition should seek formal evaluation by a mental health professional.

ISBN: 978-0-9748836-2-5

Author's Preface

When I went into the field of psychiatry, I questioned the need for psychotropic drugs. I had the hope that all mental and emotional illnesses could be treated non-medically through interventions such as guidance, support, exercise, diet, and prayer. Therefore, I set out to do just that—treat all psychiatric illnesses without the use of medication.

It would take nearly a decade of clinical experience to convince me that psychotropic medication was not only important, but in some cases, an essential part of treatment.

Today, after eighteen years and approximately fifty-six thousand hours of working with patients, I believe that the majority of severe and persistent emotional distress is the result of a neurochemical imbalance (often caused by a kind of exhaustion of the brain) and is highly responsive to medical treatment.

Despite the seriousness of mood disorders, most sufferers never seek appropriate treatment. Lack of understanding about the medical nature of these conditions prevents many persons from seeking the care that could allow them to live healthy and productive lives. For those who do seek treatment, a basic understanding of mood disorders, the signs and symptoms, and the new treatment options available can maximize the chances of receiving safe and effective treatment.

Medical progress in the area of mood disorders is occurring so rapidly that public education is lagging further and further behind advances in treatment. This book is an effort to bridge the gap between medical progress and public education about mood disorders and to give patients the information they need to help their doctors make the right diagnosis and prescribe the right treatment.

My hope is that this information will bring new hope to those who suffer from depression and help them work more effectively with their physicians and therapists toward achieving happier, healthier, and more productive lives.

To my patients,
whose courage, patience, and trust
have made the writing of this book possible...

TABLE OF CONTENTS

Desperation

It feels like a caustic liquid burning up inside of me. It expands throughout the chest until the whole chest cavity is gripped by this fiery sensation that just seems to intensify.

It is at this moment that desperation sets in. At first, it feels like a knot or butterflies in my stomach. But soon, it turns into agony. The fiery feeling of this agony and the corrosive sensation in my chest cause me to feel like my whole body is being tortured.

The desperation and caustic sensations then invade the brain. My thinking becomes distorted by the torture that just seems to intensify. At first, all I can think of is "God, please stop this. I cannot go on like this. I can't stand this anymore. Please make it go away." Of course, the pain doesn't go away; it intensifies. It is at this moment that I start pummeling, scratching, or cutting myself in an attempt to diminish or distract myself from this anguish.

This sensation of torture is a combination of sadness, hopelessness, helplessness, guilt, shame, doom, undeservedness. I feel like I don't deserve to live. The unhappiness makes me feel like a mourning individual who has just lost a loved one. The sense of doom and disaster make me feel like the only way out is to just cease to exist. Logic and rationality become distorted by the infection of the corrosive and desperate feeling. Suddenly, intruding images enter the poisoned mind; I see myself dead in the middle of the street or run over by a car; or jumping from the roof of a tall building; or setting myself on fire; or cutting my throat. At first, I might try to dismiss these images; but they keep intruding into my mind more and more until they become all-consuming.

All I want is for this torture, this anguish, to end. The pain is so great that my eyes, like opened floodgates, start to shed tears. At first, it is only a few tears; then it is wrenching, sobbing, and bawling. I want to stop, but no matter what I do, the crying continues. The level of agony and torment can only be tolerated for so long.

My thoughts become a whirlwind of confusion. Thinking is murky. I can conceive thoughts, formulate sentences, ideas…but this corrosive infection has impaired the uttering of such sentences or ideas. The only words that seem to come out are "it hurts; please make it go away; help me, or I just want to die."

This feeling of desperation, of caustic corrosion, of poison, of agony…if not stopped…will end up in the deterioration of the mind and brain, the body and soul. Without intervention, death–in one way or another–is imminent.

—experience of a patient with clinical depression.

CHAPTER 1

—◦◦◦✣◦◦◦—

OVERVIEW OF DEPRESSION

An estimated one million Americans suffer from depression. According to the World Health Organization, depression is the leading cause of disability worldwide, as measured by years lived with disability. Each year an estimated thirty thousand persons commit suicide—about one person every twenty minutes. Suicide is the second leading cause of death among females and the fourth among males. Yet the vast majority of sufferers never seek treatment. Some are not aware that something is wrong with them; others do not believe they need help; still others fear the stigma of mental illness. Of those who do seek treatment, more than one-third fail to respond to antidepressants. This book is an effort to unveil the mystery behind depression, prevent suffering, and save lives.

Depression has traditionally been viewed as a symptom of something wrong in a person's life, something that casts a shadow over his or her happiness and robs the person of energy, enthusiasm, and sometimes even the desire to live.

Through the ages depression has been assumed to be entirely psychological in nature, a sign of character weakness and inability to cope with life. However, recent advances in molecular biology, neuroimaging, and psychopharmacology have led to the discovery that depression is not always psychological. In many cases, depression is a symptom of an electrochemical abnormality in the brain. In order to understand this abnormality, one must consider the relationship between the brain and the psyche.

The human brain is a highly complex electrochemical computer. The brain forms during the sixth week of gestation under the direction of a code that the fertilized egg receives from the parents in the form

1

of deoxyribonucleic acid (DNA). As the *neurons* (the cells of the brain) are forming, their projections (called *axons* and *dendrites*) weave their way through the body, thereby integrating the brain with the arms, legs, and every organ and tissue. By the time of birth, the cells of the brain are so organized and coordinated with the subordinate systems of the body that their topography literally creates a functional drawing of the entire person. The intricate relationship between the brain and the body allows the brain, through a series of reflexes and chemical reactions, to process nearly every activity that occurs in the body.

The brain itself, however, does not think and feel; it merely computes what we think and feel. It acts as an integration and relay center between the body and the psyche or "soul."

The Human Soul

A human being is more than just a collection of DNA and cytoplasm, more than just a sack of chemical reactions and neurological reflexes. A human being is a person—a living being. This person is a living spirit–an energy body–clothed with the flesh. The head of the spirit, or "soul," animates the body and governs its behavior.

Because the soul is invisible and intangible, precious little has been written about it in scientific literature; yet we know that it exists, because we have the ability to think and feel, sometimes very vividly, even when our brains are asleep at night. This is true even when there is virtual suppression of cerebral cortical function, such as when the brain is under general anesthesia during surgery or temporarily loses function in severe head trauma or brief clinical death. Further evidence of the soul comes from a pair of Siamese twins who are conjoined at the head. They have separate bodies but one head with their faces set at an angle to each other. Despite the fact that they share the same brain, they have different likes and dislikes, and their personalities are different. Clearly, they are two different persons–two individual souls– who share the same biological computer.

Thoughts and feelings are very real even though they are not physical or measurable. Who would deny the reality of love or the existence of friendship? Although these bonds are invisible and intangible, they are important to us; indeed, they are the very essence of our being. This is true even for those who show physical evidence of brain deterioration, such as in Alzheimer's disease, cerebral vascular disease, and other dementing illnesses. Many patients with advanced disease are no longer able to interact appropriately or even acknowledge the presence of their loved ones, yet they continue to need and benefit from their emotional support.

Another point of evidence for the existence of the soul is meditation. In this ancient discipline, the soul attempts to transcend the physical world by ignoring input from the brain. The break in dialogue between the soul and the brain gives both a rest and promotes healing of mind, body, and spirit. Medical experts are becoming increasingly aware of the powerful influence that the mind has over the body in sickness and in health.

Perhaps there is no better evidence for the existence of the soul than the mysterious divide between life and death. The development of advanced life support has led to heated debates over whether a patient is alive or dead when the lungs are breathing and the heart is beating but when the patient remains unconscious for days, weeks, or months. Large medical teams and multidisciplinary ethics committees often struggle with the question of whether or not to "pull the plug." There is still no objective measure of the difference between life and death that medical experts can agree upon. The one thing they do agree upon is this: once the person is dead, the person is dead. So what is that critical difference, that mysterious divide between life and death? The answer is the soul. Once it leaves the body, the person is dead. And so we say, "he passed away."

Anatomy of the Soul

The soul is made of spirit; that is, energy and intelligence. Spirit is finer than the smallest particles that scientific instruments can measure. Therefore, the existence of the soul transcends science. Yet, more is known about the soul than the brain because moral philosophy preceded scientific observation. Moral principles have been taught and debated for thousands of years, whereas science is a relatively new field.

Because the soul is spiritual, its anatomy can best be described functionally. The soul has two natures: it has a carnal nature, and it has a moral nature. Our carnal nature is characterized by carnal instincts that help ensure our survival in the flesh. These include the perception of temperature, touch, hunger, pain, fatigue, and a variety of other sensations that help ensure our physical well-being. The emotions that these sensations produce, some of which are pleasant and others of which are unpleasant, are also part of our carnal nature.

Our moral nature is characterized by moral instincts that help us grow spiritually and survive as a society. These include honesty, patience, kindness, charity, forgiveness, and other virtues that, when practiced through the gift of will, form the basis of love. Our moral nature gives rise to peace, joy, shame, and guilt, all of which are in the service of our moral instincts, just as our carnal emotions are in the service of our carnal instincts.

Functionally then, we have two minds. The carnal mind corresponds to our carnal nature and thinks about things practically; the moral mind corresponds to our moral nature and thinks about things ethically. When the carnal mind and the moral mind are satisfied and in agreement, the soul is at ease and there is peace in the "heart" (what we consider the "eye" of the soul, the very core of our being). However, when circumstances arise that bring the carnal mind into conflict with the moral mind, the soul experiences intrapsychic tension. This phenomenon became the focus of an entire school of psychoanalytic psychotherapy pioneered by the Austrian physician Sigmund Freud. Freud developed techniques for helping people become aware of the emotional conflicts that were producing symptoms of anxiety and depression.

All of us are familiar with the negative emotions that shame, loss, and disappointment create, but recent advances in molecular biology, neuroimaging, and psychopharmacology have led to the identification of a different cause of anxiety and depression—a cause that can produce the same kinds of emotions as intrapsychic conflict but stems from an electrochemical abnormality in the brain. In order to understand this phenomenon, the relationship between the soul and the brain must be explored.

The Soul-Brain Relationship

All of our emotions, whether related to the carnal mind or the moral mind, are experienced by the soul. As the soul contemplates, emotions are produced. The substrate for these emotions is the information that the soul receives from the brain and from the spiritual world together with the information that the soul has retained from prior experiences. Although the brain itself does not "emote," it processes and stores the same information that the soul processes and stores. Thus, the brain "remembers" (neurochemically) everything that the soul thinks and feels. The brain also receives information from the body and its surroundings via an electrical network, the *peripheral nervous system*. This system of nerves allows the brain to process information in the service of the soul and act as a mediator between the soul and the environment. The relationship between the soul and the brain is comparable to that between a computer operator and a computer, in which the soul is the computer operator and the brain the computer. Figure 1 is a schematic illustration of the anatomical relationship between the soul and the brain that is based upon neurological facts and spiritual principles.

When the neurological system is functioning normally, the brain provides the soul with an appropriate representation of the environment. In some disease states, however, the neurological system malfunctions and fails to convey information properly to the soul, as, for example, in the case of a gunshot wound where the bullet has damaged the spinal chord, and neurological information is unable to get past the point of injury. In this instance, the soul can no longer receive messages from or send messages to the corresponding area of the body. As a result, the injured person experiences numbness and paralysis.

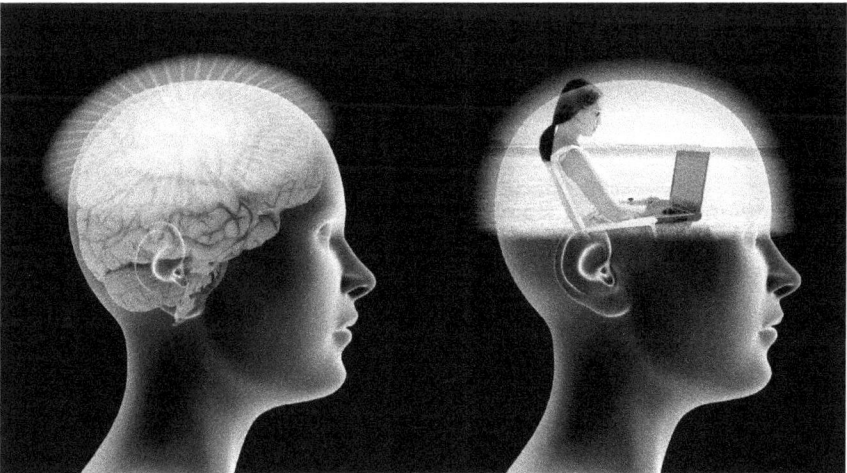

Fig. 1 The image on the left depicts the soul (bright hallow) in relationship to the brain. The image on the right illustrates the functional relationship between the soul and the brain, in which the woman represents the soul, and the computer represents the brain. Like the woman and the computer, the soul and the brain interact in a dialogue that we call the "mind."

Another example is a stroke. In this case, damage to the brain deprives the soul of the information that the affected neurons normally convey. The damage might also prevent the brain from processing information from the soul. As a result, the patient might experience difficulty moving (paralysis), understanding (receptive aphasia), speaking (expressive aphasia), or thinking (cognitive dysfunction).

An example that all of us can relate to is the leg that "falls asleep." In this instance, prolonged pressure on the sciatic nerve (the large nerve in the leg) temporarily disrupts communication between the leg and the brain. Since the brain mediates communication between the soul and the legs, we experience difficulty feeling or moving the affected leg.

Functionally, the brain and the soul are in a continuous dialogue. The brain processes information from the environment and then relays the message to the soul, which then processes the message and responds according to the dictates of the will. As the soul contemplates information from the brain, various emotions arise. In the process, sensory neurological information becomes linked to specific emotions, which are re-experienced each time the brain is exposed to the same environmental stimulus. In theory, the reverse could also occur— specific emotions could potentially reproduce the sensory phenomena to which they were originally linked.

The system of the brain that is involved in the processing of emotion is called the *limbic system*. The limbic system is a diffuse network of neuronal circuitry that is also involved in the regulation of energy, concentration, sleep, appetite, libido, and a variety of other functions that are commonly affected in mood disorders.

Under normal conditions, the brain acts as an objective mediator between the soul and the environment. Specific circuits in the brain are stimulated by descending input from the soul and by ascending input from the environment. The information is then integrated in the brain and "presented" to the soul.

In mood and anxiety disorders, an electrochemical abnormality in the brain can either exaggerate or dull emotions and can produce a variety of inappropriate emotions, perceptions, and functional abnormalities, including disturbances in sleep, appetite, energy, libido, concentration, and motivation. In more severe cases, hallucinations and delusions can occur. Some of these signs and symptoms can be chronic; others can fluctuate, depending upon the nature and severity of the neurological abnormality. In some cases, these limbic abnormalities occur spontaneously. But they can also be caused or influenced by psychosocial stressors and a variety of medical conditions, prescription drugs, and substances of abuse.

Understanding these phenomena is important because the brain exerts a powerful influence on the soul. If abnormalities in the brain are left untreated, the neurological dysfunction can cause deep emotional suffering and lead to self-neglect, social withdrawal, immorality, and other behaviors that are destructive to one's physical health, one's relationships, and one's soul.

Mood Disorders: Pathophysiology and Historical Background

As discussed earlier, the brain is a highly complex network of electrochemical circuits that serves us like a computer. Each neuron communicates with its neighbors via *neurotransmitters*, small amino acid derivatives. These chemical messengers are stored in packets and released by a wave of electrical current that travels to them via the long arm of the cell. Once released, the chemical messengers swim across the *synaptic cleft*, the small space between neurons, and stimulate the adjacent

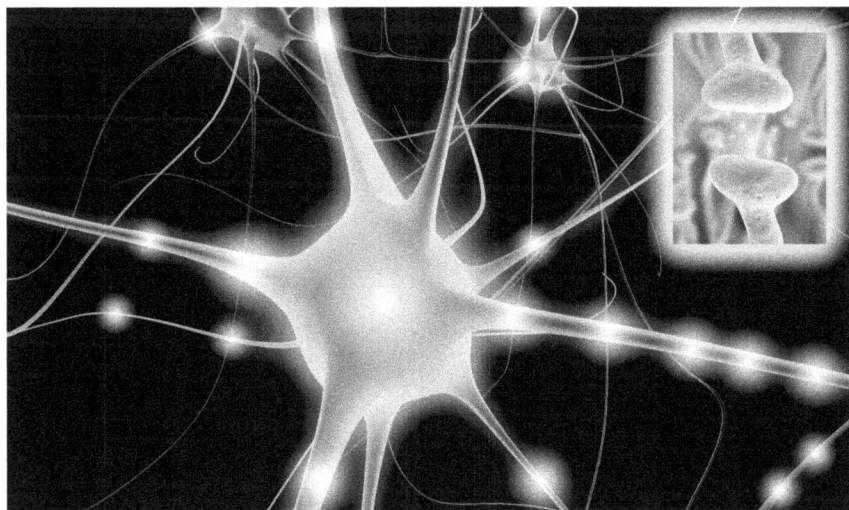

Fig. 2 Schematic illustration of one of six billion neurons in the brain and its relationship to neighboring neurons. The bright spots along the arm of the neuron represent electrical waves called *action potentials*, which stimulate the release of neurotransmitters into the synaptic cleft (inset upper right).

7

neuron. The electrical signal is produced by the depolarizing effect that neurotransmitters have on the cell membrane (Figure 2).

Over the past two decades, an extensive body of literature has accumulated that implicates the neurotransmitters *norepinephrine* and *serotonin* in the pathophysiology of mood disorders. The data come from the observation that an expanding group of medications that have been effective against mood disorders modulate the activity of norepinephrine and serotonin. In many cases, treatment with an "antidepressant" makes the patient feel better, and both the patient and the doctor are satisfied.

In recent years the pharmaceutical industry has invested a great deal of time, energy, and resources in the development of new and improved antidepressants. The fervor for this activity was generated by the success of a new antidepressant that became available in the 1980s, Prozac (fluoxetine). The success of Prozac in treating anxiety and depression spawned the production of a new line of antidepressants, *selective serotonin reuptake inhibitors (SSRIs)*.

Like Prozac, the other SSRIs were believed to exert their therapeutic effects by blocking the "reuptake" (removal) of serotonin after it is released by neurons in the limbic system, thereby increasing the activity of serotonin in the system. Because SSRIs were more selective in their effects than tricyclic antidepressants, they caused fewer side effects and, therefore, were preferred by patients. Along with the SSRIs, a number of related compounds have been approved by the Food and Drug Adminstration (FDA) for the treatment of depression. Today there are more than twenty-five antidepressants on the market.

In the midst of the excitement about antidepressants, relatively little attention had been paid to a subtype of depression called *manic-depression* (also called *bipolar disorder*). Manic-depression is clinically indistinguishable from classic (unipolar) depression when the patient is in the depressive phase of the illness. The clinical distinction between the two disorders becomes apparent only when the manic-depressive develops the signs and symptoms of mania.

Because of the difficulty in identifying a history of manic episodes, manic-depressive disorder is often misdiagnosed as unipolar depression. A 1992 survey conducted by the Depression and Bipolar Support Alliance (formerly the National Depressive and Manic-Depressive Association) found that nearly seventy-five percent of patients with manic-depressive disorder had been misdiagnosed, with unipolar depression being the most common misdiagnosis. When the survey was repeated in 2000, sixty-nine percent of respondents reported that they had initially been misdiagnosed. Many of the patients had consulted five or more physicians, and more than one-third had waited ten years or more before being diagnosed accurately. Proper diagnosis is critical because antidepressants (originally intended to treat unipolar depression) can exacerbate the symptoms of manic-depression.

Diagnosis of Classic (Unipolar) Depression

Unipolar depression is a syndrome that typically involves a gradual loss of energy, enthusiasm, motivation, and interest in one's usual activities. Other symptoms may include anxiety, irritability, poor concentration, heightened emotionality, decreased sex drive, changes in sleep, and changes in appetite. Some patients with major depression also experience physical symptoms, such as dizziness, headaches, chest pain, stomachaches, skin rash, and other symptoms that can lead to an extensive medical work-up. As symptoms progress, there is often a noticeable weight change, excessive worrying, tearfulness, social withdrawal, feelings of hopelessness, and declining ability to function at home and at work. In extreme cases, there can be a loss of the desire to live. Some patients experience just one or two of the aforementioned symptoms; others experience most or all of them. Of greater importance than the number of symptoms in making the diagnosis is their gradual onset over weeks or months without any relief despite all efforts to make things better (Figure 3).

A minority of patients have a chronic form of depression in which the symptoms persist for many years. In a fraction of these cases,

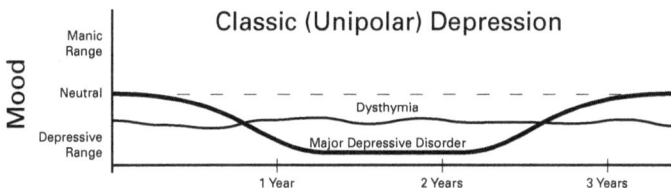

Fig. 3 Schematic illustration of the natural course of a major depressive episode (thick line) and dysthymia (thin line). Note the gradual onset of symptoms in major depression, followed by a persistence of severe symptoms with eventual return to normal functioning. In dysthymia, also known as chronic low-grade depression, depressive symptoms are less severe but more chronic in nature.

symptoms are not severe enough to meet criteria for major depressive disorder. In such cases, the diagnosis of dysthymia is given. There are also some patients who have a seasonal recurrence of symptoms. These individuals appear to be sensitive to the change of season and associated changes in sunlight. They are given a diagnosis of seasonal affective disorder (SAD).

Diagnosis of Bipolar Disorder

The diagnosis of bipolar disorder is made once an episode of mania has been identified. Mania is a syndrome that is characterized by a persistently elevated, emotionally charged, or highly agitated state that persists for at least four days. Typical symptoms include an abundance of energy with decreased sleep, racing thoughts, persistent speech, inflated self-esteem, impulsivity, distractibility, and excessive involvement in emotionally exciting activities such as grandiose business ventures, excessive spending, and sexual indiscretion. In order to qualify for the diagnosis, several (but not necessarily all) of the aforementioned symptoms must be present to a degree severe enough to markedly impair social and occupational functioning. Some bipolar patients never experience mania but do experience a mild form of the syndrome, called *hypomania*, in which case the diagnosis of bipolar II disorder is given.

In patients with bipolar disorder, periods of mania or hypomania typically alternate with periods of depression. In the process, the patient's behavior and emotions oscillate from one polar extreme to the other; hence the term "bipolar." In some cases, the change in symptoms can be so sudden and dramatic that persons with the disorder have been referred to as "Dr. Jekyll and Mr. Hyde." In contrast, unipolar depressives do not experience any significant fluctuation of symptoms.

Bipolar Spectrum Disorder: an Emerging Diagnosis

In recent years, there has been a trend toward recognizing milder and less typical forms of bipolar disorder such as cyclothymia, cyclic depression, depressive mixed states, and hyperthymic temperament.

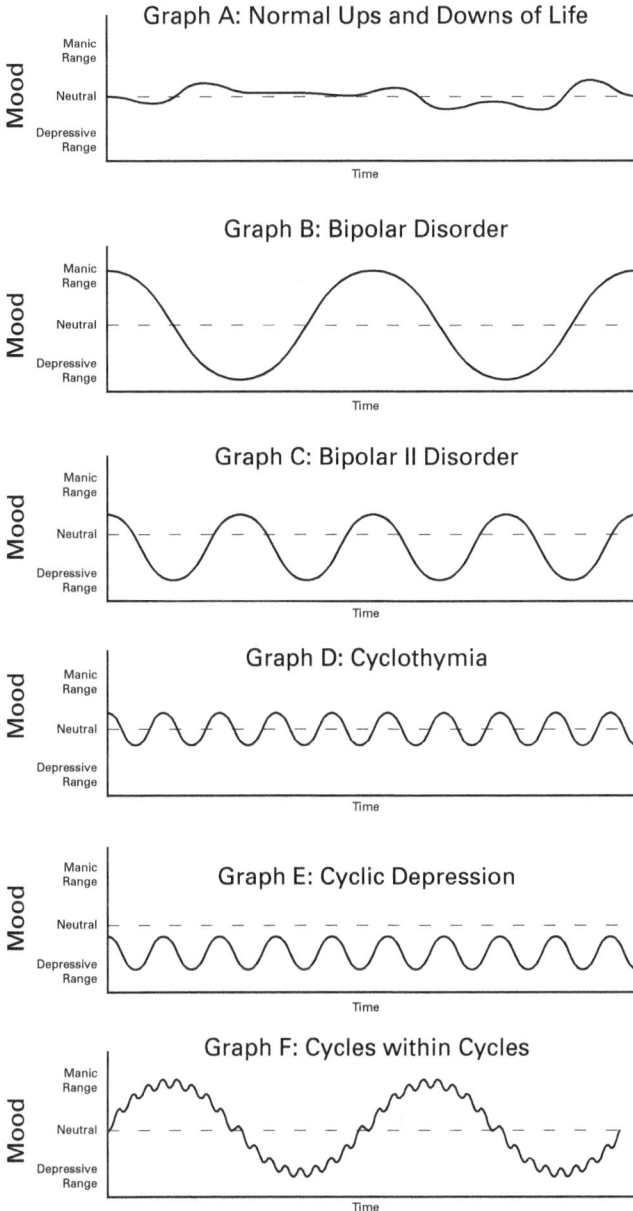

Fig. 4 Schematic illustration of the various forms that a cyclic mood disorder can take in comparison to the normal ups and downs of life. Graph A: normal ups and downs of life; graph B: bipolar disorder; graph C: bipolar II disorder; graph D: cyclothymia; graph E: cyclic depression; graph F: cycles within cycles. Note that in comparison to the normal "ups and downs of life," the pattern in cyclic mood disorders is sinusoidal and exaggerated.

Cyclothymia is characterized by periods of hypomania alternating with periods of depression that are not severe enough to meet criteria for major depressive episode. Cyclic depression is characterized by depressive symptoms that wax and wane in severity but never completely subside. Depressive mixed states are characterized by classic symptoms of depression accompanied by marked anxiety, irritability, and racing thoughts. Hyperthymic temperament is an emotionally charged state that characterizes the long-term functioning of a person. Persons with hyperthymic temperament tend to be extremely outgoing and ambitious but are at risk for extremes in behavior that can lead to serious social and financial problems. They are also at increased risk of becoming anxious and depressed. The similarity of these conditions to bipolar disorder suggests that they may be mild forms of the disorder (Figure 4). In recognition of this relationship, cyclothymia, cyclic depression, depressive mixed states, and hyperthymic temperament have been referred to collectively as "bipolar spectrum disorder."

The length of time between affective states in bipolar spectrum disorder is highly variable and can range from minutes to hours (in the most rapid cycling forms) to days to weeks (in the slower cycling forms). The most common form is ultra-rapid cycling, in which cycles last several hours to several days. Many persons have cycles within cycles, wherein there is ultra-rapid cycling of some symptoms superimposed upon longer periods of other symptoms (Figure 4-Graph F).

Because of the intermittent nature of their symptoms, most persons with bipolar spectrum disorder do not realize that they have heightened emotionality and exaggerated responses to psychological cues. However, a number of common features can help bipolar patients and their families draw the distinction between normal emotions and the symptoms that characterize disorders in the bipolar spectrum. Following are some of the more subtle signs and symptoms of bipolarity:

- A pattern of enthusiasm and high productivity that frequently gives way to apathy and low productivity.
- Periods of excitement, high energy, and talkativeness that are out of proportion to the psychosocial circumstances of one's life. This could include excessive confidence, flirtatiousness, spending, and risk taking, with little thought about the potential consequences of such thinking and behavior. During this time, family and friends might

notice that the person is not acting his or her normal self.

- Periods of sadness or depression that begin either spontaneously or as an overreaction to life stressors, and then persist for minutes, hours, or days, before resolving either spontaneously or as a reaction to a positive life event.
- A pattern of "good days" and "bad days" that may alternate or occur unpredictably.
- A sense of uncertainty or unpredictability about how one is going to feel or what mood one is going to be in from minute to minute, hour to hour, day to day, or week to week.
- A pattern of inconsistency and unpredictability in one's reaction to life events.
- A pattern of randomly occurring nervousness, anxiety, or irritability with or without a clearly discernible precipitant.
- Episodes of anger that occur suddenly and unpredictably and about which one is later remorseful or embarrassed.
- Marked fluctuations in energy, appetite, or sex drive that occur intermittently and without reason.
- Periods of poor concentration alternating with periods when concentration seems normal or exceptionally good.
- Racing thoughts that may be intermittent or persistent and may cause one to feel as if one's mind will not "shut off." These thoughts, either positive or negative, may interfere with concentration; they may also interfere with the ability to sleep.
- A sense of not being in control of one's thoughts. This feeling might include having intrusive thoughts and thoughts that are odd, inappropriate, or embarrassing.
- A pattern of instability in interpersonal relationships or job performance or both, with a tendency to move from one relationship to another or from one job to another.
- An intermittent feeling of being "in a fog," "losing one's mind," or "going crazy."
- Alterations in perception, such as increased sensitivity to light, sound, or pain that either comes and goes or varies in intensity.
- Intermittent feelings of being overwhelmed and unable to cope with life.

Note that the essential feature in cyclic mood disorders is a pattern of *alternating* or *intermittent* symptoms. Clinical experience has shown that the inconsistency and variability of symptoms is more important than the nature of the symptoms in distinguishing bipolar disorders from other conditions with which symptoms of anxiety and depression can be associated. The other important diagnostic feature of bipolar disorders is extremes of emotion that are inconsistent with or out of proportion to environmental cues.

Distinguishing one form of depression from another is crucial to diagnosis and treatment. Patients can help lead their doctors to an accurate diagnosis by preparing a brief written or oral summary of their history, including their primary symptoms, the approximate time course over which they developed, and any tendency for their symptoms to come and go or to alternate. Because the cyclic form nearly always begins during late childhood, the development of symptoms around adolescence is virtually diagnostic.

Pathophysiology of Mood Disorders

Despite numerous research studies on mood disorders and dozens of medications available to treat them, the precise nature of the neurological abnormality remains unclear. The old monoamine hypothesis held that relative neurotransmitter depletion led to the development of symptoms that were reversed by medications that normalized the concentration of norepinephrine and serotonin in the synaptic cleft. However, this did not explain the two to six-week delay in treatment response that was typically seen with antidepressants.

The current hypothesis is that antidepressants create an immediate rise in the concentration of monoamines in the synaptic cleft but that the system compensates for a period of time, thus explaining the delay in treatment response. In bipolar disorder, alternating symptoms of mania and depression are thought to arise from neuronal changes that lead to an alternating pattern of overrelease and underrelease of monoamines.

The current hypothesis has developed under the assumption that unipolar depression and bipolar disorder are neurologically distinct conditions. However, the idea that the two disorders are different does not explain why unipolar depression and bipolar disorder share many of the same characteristics, nor does it explain why they often respond to the same treatment. The hypothesis also fails to take into consideration the functional circuitry of the brain.

Contrary to the current view, a growing body of literature suggests that unipolar depression and bipolar disorder are actually opposite ends of a bipolar spectrum and might be caused by the same neurological abnormality. This view much better explains a number of phenomena that are commonly observed in treatment; namely, that unipolar depression and bipolar disorder share many of the same symptoms; that one disorder can evolve into the other; and that the two disorders respond to many of the same treatments, including antidepressants, antipsychotics, and electroconvulsive therapy (ECT).

Based on the latest scientific data and years of treating mood disorders, my theory is that *neuronal membrane hyperexcitability* is the fundamental abnormality underlying the spectrum of disorders from unipolar depression to bipolar disorder. Over the last decade, approaching depression from this perspective has nearly doubled my treatment success with patients. The details of the *multicircuit neuronal hyperexcitability (MCNH) hypothesis* are discussed in a separate scientific article, but the essence of it is discussed here in order to prepare the reader for the case examples that follow.

The MCNH hypothesis contends that depression, mania, and mixed emotional states are the result of hyperexcitability of neurons in brain circuits that are associated with these syndromes. For example, hyperexcitability of neurons in circuits that are associated with dysphoria could create a depressive state, while hyperexcitability of neurons in circuits that are associated with pleasure could create a manic state. Hyperexcitability in both types of circuits simultaneously could create mixed states of mania and depression. The length, the pattern, and severity of these syndromes would depend on the duration and degree of neuronal hyperexcitability. In some cases, neurons in circuits for anxiety and depression could become and remain hyperexcitable for a lengthy period, thereby giving rise to a major depressive episode. In other cases, neurons in various circuits could rapidly oscillate in and out of hyperexcitability thereby giving rise to ultra-rapid-cycling bipolar disorder, cyclothymia, and other syndromes in the bipolar spectrum.

If we think back to Figure 1, experiencing a mood disorder is like working on a computer that is not functioning properly. Instead of accurately receiving and computing information, the brain (like a malfunctioning computer) is ignoring some of the input, corrupting the data, and producing information that has not been requested. This creates cognitive and emotional chaos for the affected individual. The neuronal hyperactivity and associated intrapsychic stress create surges of emotion that cause the mind to churn like a tornado, as depicted in Figure 5.

Because the brain is influenced by the soul, intrapsychic stress could fuel the electrical problem described above. Conversely, a healthy attitude and good coping skills could help reduce the symptoms by reducing intrapsychic stress. However, the fundamental abnormality appears to be genetic and independent of one's personality, attitude, or degree of maturity. Some of the world's greatest names have struggled with mood disorders, Sir Isaac Newton, Ludwig Van Beethoven, Abraham Lincoln, Michelangelo Buonarroti, Buzz Aldren.

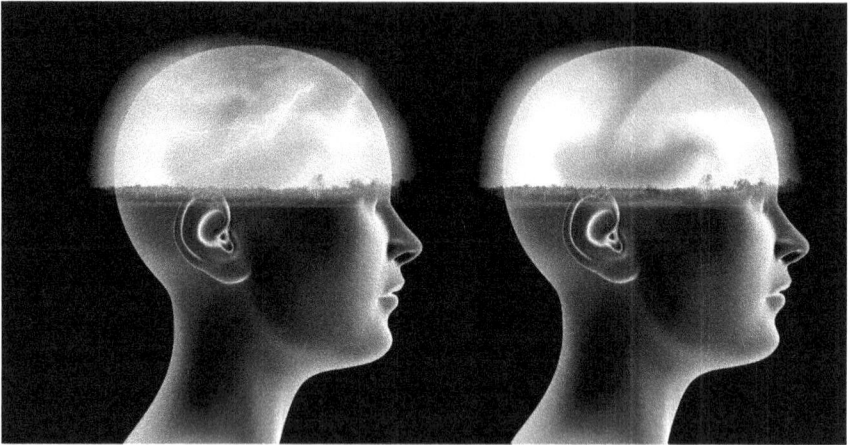

Fig. 5 The electrical storm in the image on the left represents neuronal hyperexcitability in the brain. The tornado illustrated in the image on the right represents the devastating effect that hyperexcitable circuits can have on one's emotions and one's life. In unipolar depressive disorders, the tornado theoretically remains in one place, involving one type of emotional circuit and producing one kind of depressive emotion. In bipolar disorders, the tornado theoretically roams from one type of emotional circuit to another, thereby producing the waves of emotion that characterize syndromes in the bipolar spectrum. In both types of disorders, as in nature, more than one tornado (hyperactive circuit) can exist and persist simultaneously, creating combinations of different emotions. Also as in nature, there tend to be more tornados in the brain at the change of season because the brain is a part of nature and is affected by the same seasonal phenomena.

+ + +

CHAPTER 2

— ⚜ —

A CASE OF BIPOLAR DISORDER
THROUGH THE EYES OF THE PATIENT

Testimonial

I want to say, before I get into the specifics, that what I am writing about is my experience and may not be the same or even similar to others in my position. I have respect for the individual struggle we all face to fit into both our own souls and the world and would never presume to say that I had it harder or worse than anyone else. Emotional pain cannot be compared; each of us can know deep love, joy, despair, and hope. We know them intimately, and what we do to express their depth, their power within, is completely our own.

The day I decided to take my own life, all the things they told us in school about suicide I found to be true. I became calm, very calm. The world looked as if I were watching it through a mesh screen, separate and broken. I felt as if I was stuck in a beautiful light gray cloud; I could not move my legs or arms or my head; I could not speak or even cry. I remember staring at the ceiling, numb. It was January, a dark day, and what I remember comes to me in flashes instead of memories. I arranged my medication next to me; I cut lines horizontally on my inner arm and arranged the blankets around me, so I was surrounded by softness, by the soft world I couldn't stand one more minute.

When I was a little girl, I talked to God quite a bit. Most of it silly child-talk, but I can honestly say I always received an answer. There has always been a voice on the inside of me with answers for my questions, and I believe it to be the voice of God. As I grew up, I had a difficult time accepting God as a part of a world that judged my choices, put value in material possessions, and had a hand in the general struggle that seemed to accompany every minute of the day. I tied Him to the good and bad things that happened to me, and it caused me to distance myself. The voice faded, and my ability to trust anyone's desire to help virtually vanished. I was diagnosed with depression when I was eighteen, and since my father had had it as well as my grandfather, it came as no surprise. I was put on Prozac, and the sadder I got, the higher the dosage I was given. I stopped taking it about three years in; all I felt were these terrible side effects. I don't know what I expected the medication to do, but I also wasn't told what to expect.

I had to go back on medication when I was twenty-five; I had developed anorexia and the habit of cutting myself. I had never been so lost in my life. My skin, my body, was damaged, but the deepest damage was in my heart. The only thing I truly believed in was despair. At that point I held such a level of comfort with sadness, the true risk was not whether I would commit suicide, but why I would fight to change something that gave me comfort. When a person is at this place, and I feel it is vitally important to describe how dangerously far the human psyche as well as the soul can fall, there seem to be few choices. I was always aware that there was an ultimate choice, but the entire world was a hole that was filled with fear, fear of moving or trying anything new, let alone recovering. A normal life, or what we would think of as a normal life, was so far away that it seemed truly impossible. All that was real was the cocoon I created, which trapped me in its warmth.

And where was God? That's how I thought of it: "Where are you God, when I am suffering so much? How can you not see me here in my bed, bleeding and intent on taking my own life?" It is important to say that I did not blame God for the terrible place I was, but I did blame Him for not saving me. Does this make sense? I logically knew that He did not cause my suffering—no one thing did—but couldn't He save me from the pain? Depression was too big for me; it had developed from situations, chemistry, and circumstances I couldn't control and yet completely controlled my life, affected every area, and left so much destruction behind.

There I was, sitting in my bed, staring at the ceiling. I felt safe, knowing that I was going to die; I was happy that the weight was going to be lifted. There was a phone right next to my bed, on the same nightstand where the pills sat. I reached over and honestly don't remember much after that until there were two policemen at my front door. I had called the hospital instead of taking the pills and had spoken to a man at the behavioral unit who had in turn called the police to pick me up. I don't think I need to get into what made me call instead of taking the pills; everyone at some point in life has an unexplained miracle that only that person knows and understands intimately. The event really did show me that I was not alone, and that's what I took from that day; even if the feeling of being totally alone was still there, by no means that was true. The police took me to the hospital, and it was in the back of a police car on my way to a mental hospital that I knew I would live. I can still hear the policemen talking to me, trying to be so sensitive and understanding. I can still feel the hard plastic seat beneath me and see the metal grid separating us. Everything from that moment on I can remember vividly—my fourteen-day stay at the hospital and, in particular, the moment I knew God was beside me in my decision to recover.

I was sitting outside the recreational room the second day I was there, when a man approached me, introduced himself, and told me that he was going to be my doctor from that point on. I didn't care, I didn't care about anything, but certainly not who was going to be treating me. I was so discouraged with the doctors I had had in the past, they seemed to be nervous around me or unwilling to ask what questions I really needed to answer, but I followed him to one of the smaller discussion rooms, and we began to talk about what had led up to this hospital stay. And I mean EVERYTHING that led up to it, from the very beginning. He asked very specific questions; and while I don't remember them all, I do remember what feeling came over me as he spoke. It was wave after wave of what felt like…forgiveness. When the tight feeling in the chest unravels and expands to its normal size, forgiveness. Forgiveness for myself, for all the terrible things I had done to myself, forgiveness for shutting the door on life, forgiveness for blocking a relationship with my spirituality. I knew it wasn't just the man I was talking to; I felt that he was a messenger, and even though I had already decided to live, to struggle with life with or without the help of others, God was there. He forgave me for trying to destroy myself. It was then that I cried. I cried deeply and for a long time, and every time I thought I didn't have anything left, there was more.

One would think that that was all it took to get better. But as profound as that moment was for me, what lay ahead was the fight of my life, for my life. Because I had accepted the help of my doctor, there was a trust between us that I can honestly say I have never had with another person. I trusted him completely to find a way inside that awful sadness, to grasp my hand and help me to the surface of such a tremendous black hole. He never gave up; he never even showed signs of frustration or fatigue. His direct participation in my recovery repaired so many bridges broken inside me, I'm not even sure he knows how many. My doctor is the kind of person who, when he walks into the room, fills it with light. This is not a Hallmark flowery statement, nor was such a feeling conveyed during our sessions. His connection to God, to Jesus Christ, is a tangible thing—a tangible thing. If you have ever been in the presence of such a person, you know exactly what I mean. He brings forward truth, gently, about choices, emotions, behaviors, and the reality of the outside world without bitterness or helplessness. Pearl Bailey once wrote, "You never find yourself until you face the truth," and that is the door my doctor opened. The truth. I was facing my actions, facing the triggers for those actions, facing each ugly truth about myself that I usually had buried in unhealthy behaviors.

Armed with truth and trust, we began my search for a medication to bring me even further into my own healing. For me, a hard part of depression was how disconnected I had been from the day-to-day world. I couldn't concentrate, my memory was terrible, I isolated myself from everything and everyone, and to try to reconnect was impossible with this huge roadblock, partially because I wasn't sure that I wanted to reconnect. As I mentioned earlier, sadness can be a very comfortable blanket to sleep under if you let it be. I didn't want to be sad, but I didn't know if I had the energy to let a whole bunch of people in who could disappoint me, or break my heart, or ask things of me I couldn't give.

We tried, I believe, different combinations of about seven medications. They included Neurontin, Depakote, Trileptal, Wellbutrin, Topamax, and Seroquel, among others. I was being treated for a cyclical mood disorder, and my doctor was trying to pull me out of the depression by normalizing my mood with one of the mood stabilizers. Needless to say, my body was one big pulsating side effect for about a year. I felt like a puppet. This was a difficult time, too, for different reasons. I was almost useless physically because I was always reacting to various medications. Half the time I didn't even know where the heck I was or who I was. During that time, my appointments with my doctor were an anchor. They allowed me to focus clearly on my goals and progress, even when progress consisted only of gaining hope. Each time I would enter his office, a weight was lifted from my shoulders, and the fog cleared. I believe we were able to make progress at that point because we were essentially getting to know my particular mental disability well enough to find the best way to treat it. I charted my moods during the week, during the day, every hour, and every minute. He asked me to pay attention to my surroundings, what triggered sadness more than anything else, at what time of the day it was the worst for me, how many times I was still cutting myself...basically what external and internal conditions contributed to my mental well-being.

It was this focus on the concrete that made me open doors, made me want to open doors to the world around me. I saw this picture, a bigger picture, and was able from there to create my own picture, one where I was actively involved in the landscapes, the sky, the sunshine, and grass. It gave me a sense of power, a surge of energy, and what felt like strength...hope. How hard I was working was showing up in my soul, the reconditioning of my mind to accept all the existing wonderful relationships and gifts was such a daily struggle, but did make a difference. These were feelings foreign to my heart, but I welcomed them back like old friends. I've come to understand and profoundly respect that return to innocence backed by wisdom, not by youth. I had given away innocence in favor of disdain and disappointment; the moment I knew I could come back to childlike faith with the experience of age represented the next step in healing. That was a gift that the physical world could not give me; it had to come with my relationship with God and how I got to know Him again through the voice in my head, through what I learned about Jesus' struggles, through risking disappointment to allow myself to feel the emotions I had previously avoided with self-destructive habits. It was a gift I accepted from God.

After about a year I found that a small dose of an antidepressant along with a small dose of mood stabilizer made me feel not so up and down all the time. Wellbutrin and Topamax were the two that stabilized me the most. Everyone has heard the statement, "a band-aid as opposed to a cure." Previous doctors had piled one medication on top of another, possibly hoping that an "up" feeling from antidepressants would diffuse any need to deal with the outside triggers. I believe it to be absolutely necessary to work with your spirit as well as your body when you are dealing with something as strong and terrible as depression. You must come to a level of understanding about who you are in relation to the world, to a greater Being, to yourself. Maybe it was because both my parents were social workers, I found that most social workers just weren't a help to me, very textbook oriented and not engaged in my personal struggle. But my doctor was practical, seeking to improve my day-to-day concentration and memory, and then decrease my medication to the lowest effective dose. At the same time, he wanted to develop thoroughly my sense of place, to encourage my reunion with ultimate truth, and just to be there for me during the emotional turmoil that would naturally accompany this self-awareness.

It was then, when I felt capable again, capable of being a human being with deep human emotions, that I had to start repairing my understanding of God, my understanding of reality and how to deal with it. I had to find a way to fit, to allow myself to be true to who I am while living in a world that can be pretty cruel. I had been focused on changing myself to fit in, instead of adjusting to the world around me and accepting it when I couldn't adjust. I knew, logically, that life was hard for everyone; but whereas I had previously fought that reality tooth and nail, I worked on becoming positive about what was positive, around me and within.

If there is one lesson that I would like to convey by writing this, it is that I could not get better until I made that decision to fight. Depression is and can be a biochemical disease, in that it many times is not in our control. But we are in control of our battle, the way we fight, and what weapons we choose, if we make it to the front line and if we charge forward. Every day we must choose this, not just once. All the cards do not simply fall into place. Every day we have to decide to get out of bed, go to our jobs, relate with people both familiar and unfamiliar, come home, make dinner, do laundry, clean the dishes, and still hang onto a meaningful existence. Once I decided to fight, there were more roads, more decisions, but it was never as hard or as painful as when I couldn't care less if I lived or died. Everything I did to move closer to recovery—taking the medication consistently, being honest with myself and my doctor about progress, accepting backslides and trying again—were examples of the hard work that is faith. The realization that I needed help and would have to open myself to others was scary; but when I did, the person I had opened myself up to helped me save my own life. And if I hadn't, I would have missed what God has told me is in store for me: love, happiness, and a foundation that will not be rocked by small storms or tremendous ones, and the trust in myself to weather it all.

+ + +

CHAPTER 3

—⊱♦⊰—

THE MANY FACES OF
BIPOLAR DISORDER

B ecause the symptoms of bipolarity can be so subtle and varied, they frequently go unrecognized and untreated. In the vast majority of cases, the sufferers, as well as their friends and family members, assume that life stressors are the cause of the emotional pain and inconsistent behavior that the disorder causes. In an effort to increase the recognition and treatment of bipolarity, the varied symptoms, expressions, and forms of the disorder will be discussed.

EXPRESSION ONE

Bipolarity Masquerading as
"Typical Adolescence"

Although persons with cyclic mood disorders are, in all likelihood, born with the underpinnings of the disorder, they tend not to develop identifiable symptoms until late childhood or early adolescence. Bipolar disorder, the most widely known and most severe form of cyclic mood disorder, is believed to be genetically linked, but has multiple possible modes of inheritance. Psychosocial stress also seems to play a role in determining whether or not and to what degree the symptoms of the disorder will be expressed.

Among psychiatric illnesses, cyclic mood disorders are the most poorly understood. To date there is no single theory that can explain the wide variety of symptoms and rapid changes in mood, temperament, energy, concentration, and other psychological and biological functions that characterize disorders in the bipolar spectrum. In my opinion, persons with a cyclic mood disorder have a genetic tendency for neurons in the limbic system of the brain to become hyperexcitable. According to the theory, the nature of the symptoms corresponds to the type of circuit or circuits in the brain that are hyperexcitable at any point in time. For example, if neurons in depressive circuits become hyperexcitable, the person will begin to feel sad and depressed; conversely, if neurons in pleasure circuits become hyperexcitable, the person will become hopeful and optimistic.

Although the polar extremes of depression and mania have for decades been the sinequanon of bipolar disorder, experts in the field are rapidly coming to realize that they are just the tip of the iceberg in the gamut of emotional extremes that persons with cyclic mood disorders experience. In reality, most affected persons experience extremes in a variety of other emotions as well, including anxiety, irritability, and fear that can rapidly shift to feelings of confidence, excitement, and creativity. They can also experience various combinations of these emotions, even if they are contradictory and inconsistent with the person's psychosocial environment. Thus, the emotional life of the individual with a cyclic mood disorder is influenced more by which circuits in his brain are hyperexcitable than by what is happening in his life. That is not to say that he has no control over himself, but rather that his control is limited and highly dependent upon which signals his brain is sending him at any given time.

In order to help conceptualize this phenomenon, let us compare the relationship between the soul and the brain to that between a pianist and a piano, in which the pianist is the soul, and the piano is the brain. What the pianist plays is influenced by his mood, and what he plays reinforces that mood. Now let us say that high notes correspond to feeling happy, low notes correspond to feeling sad, and the various combinations thereof correspond to the various shades of emotion that all of us experience. Naturally, the piano makes no sound unless the pianist strikes a key. Likewise, the brain of a normal person produces no emotion unless the soul stimulates it via a thought or feeling. However, in the person with a mood disorder, the piano (brain) is playing without the pianist striking the keys—the brain is producing thoughts and feelings without being told to do so. The person experiences this phenomenon as a lack of control over his emotions. Those with unipolar depression continuously hear low notes that they have not played; whereas, those with manic-depression hear both high notes and low notes that sometimes alternate, sometimes merge, and sometimes fade. Thus, for the person with a mood disorder, what is being played is not a melody that reflects his mood, but emotional chaos that is out of his control. Worse yet, the volume of each note is magnified, which makes life even more disconcerting.

Yet because parents, teachers, and many health care professionals tend to overlook mood disorders, a young person's emotional difficulties are often misattributed to problems at home or at school. Under the assumption that the problem is rooted in the soul, treatment is usually limited to psychosocial interventions such as individual and family counseling. In reality, dysfunctional family dynamics, psychosocial stressors, and lack of emotional support are more apt to cause emotionally immature behavior, such as lying, delinquency, and sexual promiscuity, than clinical depression. Most young persons use psychological defense mechanisms and other coping strategies relatively well as long as their brains are functioning normally. On the other hand, routine activities and the smallest stressors can become overwhelming when the brain is not functioning normally and is distorting the messages it receives from the soul and the environment.

Unfortunately, even when a mood or anxiety disorder is suspected, the incorrect diagnosis is often made. In my experience, nearly all adolescents who present with symptoms of a mood disorder have the cyclic form. Yet the majority of them are misdiagnosed as having major depression or dysthymia and treated with antidepressants. This is problematic because antidepressants increase neurotransmission in circuits that are already overactive in cyclic mood disorders. Overstimulation of these circuits can worsen symptoms of depression and increase the risk of suicide.

According to the MCNH hypothesis, antidepressants stimulate pleasurable circuits in the brain by increasing the availability of norepinehrine and serotonin in those circuits; however, in cyclic mood disorders, the locus of hyperexcitability can shift to dysphoric circuits (the tornado can move), resulting in a sudden and unexpected return of depressive symptoms.

Not surprisingly then, antidepressants have repeatedly been observed to have a potent, but not always sustained effect upon symptoms of anxiety and depression. In patients with cyclic mood disorders, symptoms tend to recur within days, weeks, or months following the initiation of antidepressant therapy; and when they return, they can be even more severe than before the medication was started because of the excitatory effect of antidepressants. This phenomenon is referred to in the psychiatric literature as "switching."

Nevertheless, the rapid improvement in mood and energy that many patients experience with the initiation of antidepressant therapy leads them to believe that the treatment is appropriate. Consequently, the antidepressant is often overlooked as a contributor to mood instability when depressive symptoms suddenly and unexpectedly return. Instead of suspecting that the medication is ineffective, patients tend to assume that the return of symptoms is due to some psychological stressor. Hence, they are more apt to blame themselves or others than the medication. And if they are in psychotherapy, they are more apt to bring the matter to the attention of their therapist than to their prescribing physician.

Similarly, if a child or adolescent were initially resistant to taking medication, as many of them are, his or her wish to discontinue the medication due to its loss of effect is often misinterpreted by parents as a lack of compliance. Consequently, many young persons are not supported in their wishes to discontinue their antidepressant medication, particularly if it initially appeared to be effective.

Among the newer antidepressants, those with the greatest risk of having an inconsistent or paradoxical effect are Effexor (venlefaxine) and Paxil (paroxetine). In light of the association between treatment with these two antidepressants and a worsening of depressive symptoms, the FDA has recommended that children under the age of eighteen not be treated with either one of them. With regard to the other antidepressants on the market, the FDA has required drug companies to include strong (black box) safety warnings in their package insert. In December 2006, the FDA expanded these warnings to young adults. In the United Kingdom, antidepressants have been banned from use in children and adolescents.

Because bipolar spectrum disorder is such a common cause of severe emotional distress developing in late childhood and early adolescence, the condition should be suspected in every young person who becomes suicidal or requires psychiatric hospitalization. Unlike their adult counterparts, children and adolescents have not developed the coping skills to manage the rapid mood swings and varied symptoms that characterize disorders in the bipolar spectrum, nor do they have as much reverence for life and fear of death as adults do. This places them at greater risk for suicide.

CLINICAL CASE VIGNETTE

Sixteen-year-old female with delinquent behavior and anger outbursts

This bright, energetic, attractive young woman was a model child until her early teens. Prior to the beginning of high school, she was an excellent student, had lots of friends, and practiced ballet. At home, she enjoyed cooking with her mother, having friends over, and playing with her ferret.

Shortly after her twelfth birthday, she began to show signs of irritability and social withdrawal. Initially, Sara's parents thought her behavior might be due to the stress of the move they had made when Sara's father, a professional hockey player, was traded to another team. But rather than make the expected adjustment, Sara's behavior became increasingly disruptive and unpredictable. At times she would begin to cry for no reason; at other times, she would become argumentative over seemingly trivial things. Although she still showed flashes of her happy self, Sara was changing into someone her parents did not know. Was it adolescence? Was it hormones? Was it the stress of having to start high school in a new community?

During her freshman year, Sara's mood and behavior continued to be erratic. By the end of the school year, she was hanging out with a delinquent group of peers, smoking cigarettes, and failing her classes. Despite her parents' repeated attempts to redirect her, Sara seemed bent on destruction.

Over the summer, Sara began to experiment with marijuana and was frequently violating her curfew. When she was confronted about this, she would become defensive and often blow up in a rage. Although she would, at times, later apologize for her behavior, her childhood innocence seemed all but lost, and her parents did not know what to do.

Out of desperation, they sought the help of the school guidance counselor. Although they were somewhat relieved to find that their daughter's behavior was not uncommon for kids her age, they remained worried and confused about the abrupt change in Sara's attitude and behavior. After a lengthy meeting with Sara, the counselor recommended some changes in academic programming and a formal psychological evaluation.

The psychologist felt that Sara was having difficulty adjusting to the family's recent move and her new school, and so she recommended weekly psychotherapy. Although Sara was uninterested at first, she eventually took a liking to her therapist. During the course of treatment, she began to talk about her feelings and was eventually able to say that she often felt anxious and depressed. She told her therapist she had lost the self-confidence she once had and was coming to feel increasingly negative about herself. Consequently, she had become willing to compromise her values in order to be accepted by her peers. Although this brought her the attention she desired, her lack of integrity would often result in the very thing she feared—abandonment by her friends. In her efforts to please one friend, she would often offend another. In order to soothe her emotional pain, she had started smoking cigarettes and, more recently, had begun smoking marijuana and drinking alcohol.

Despite weekly sessions with her therapist, Sara's problems continued. During her second year of high school, she discovered that her boyfriend was cheating on her. When she confronted him about this, he accused her of flirting with other guys. This sent Sara into a rage, both because she felt that she was falsely accused and because her boyfriend was the one person whom she felt she could trust. The subsequent break-up put Sara in a state of severe anxiety and depression. Feeling trapped and overwhelmed, she went home to her room and began cutting her wrist with a razor blade. When her mother saw her, she called 911, and Sara was taken to the hospital by emergency services.

Due to concerns about her safety, Sara was admitted to the hospital and was seen by a psychiatrist. After interviewing Sara, the doctor met with her parents and discussed the case with her psychologist. He felt that Sara was suffering from a mood disorder in addition to the stress of the break-up. Therefore, he prescribed the antidepressant Paxil. He discussed the potential side effects of the medication and encouraged Sara to participate in group psychotherapy sessions and one-to-one meetings with the nursing staff on the psychiatric unit. He also recommended that Sara have a chemical dependency evaluation.

The combination of medication and social support that Sara received over the next several days in the hospital helped her feel much better, and she was discharged with a recommendation to follow-up with her psychiatrist and with her therapist.

During the first several days after discharge, Sara remained in good spirits; but within a few weeks, she started to feel anxious and depressed again. At Sara's first follow-up visit, the psychiatrist increased the Paxil from 20mg per day to 40mg per day.

After the medication change, Sara's depression again lifted, but her anxiety remained high. At her next office visit, Klonopin (clonazepam) was added for anxiety. The combination of Paxil and Klonopin kept Sara's symptoms in check until approximately two months later, when she lapsed back into depression. Feeling hopeless, she stopped taking her medications and began to use alcohol and marijuana again. She also stopped going to class.

While absent from school, Sara began spending time with a young man who had dropped out of high school. The new relationship lifted her spirits for a while, but before long, her anxiety and depression returned and the relationship turned stormy. Sara's new boyfriend started telling his friends about Sara's moody and unpredictable behavior, and a rumor began that Sara was "psycho." The pain of this launched her into a series of brief sexual relationships that further stained her reputation and her self-image. She eventually attempted to take her life again, this time by drug overdose, and she was readmitted to the hospital.

During the hospitalization, Sara was seen by a different doctor, who took note of her inconsistent response to the antidepressant medication and the cyclic nature of her anxiety and depression. He told Sara and her parents that she might be suffering from cyclic depression rather than classic depression. Cyclic depression, he explained, was like bipolar disorder, but not as extreme. There are no manic episodes in cyclic depression, although there might be periods of racing thoughts, anxiety, and depression. These periods, which can range in duration from minutes to hours to weeks, are often followed by a period of relatively normal functioning. The doctor explained that the disorder generally begins sometime before the age of twenty-one; most commonly, during early adolescence.

This, thought Sara's parents, would explain why Sara had gone from model child to troubled teenager in just a year's time. The doctor explained that the disorder tends to be overlooked because many of the symptoms, such as moodiness, irritability, and defiance are misattributed to "normal adolescence." Although some degree of stubbornness and defiance are a normal part of a teenager's transition into adulthood, normal adolescent behavior is not as disruptive, self-defeating, and unpredictable as Sara's behavior had been. The doctor further explained that because cyclic mood disorders involve an electrochemical abnormality of the brain, they should be treated medically. He discussed the types of medication available and explained that several different mood stabilizers might need to be tried before an effective one could be found.

Feeling reassured by the doctor's thoughtful explanation and almost telepathic understanding of her symptoms, Sara agreed to a trial of *mood stabilizers* (more aptly called mood normalizers). The first medication he prescribed was Keppra (levetiracetam). After several doses without improvement, the doctor discontinued it, explaining that mood stabilizers usually work either immediately or not at all. Next, Neurontin (gabapentin) was tried. After two days on the medication, Sara began to notice that her anxiety had markedly diminished and that she was feeling more stable and grounded. After a total of five days on the medication, the dosage was doubled, and Sara experienced further improvement.

As the medication took effect, Sara stopped arguing with her parents and began to behave more predictably. Her attendance at school began to improve, and her grades rebounded. Almost as quickly as she had left, the old Sara had returned. The therapeutic effects of the medication also allowed her to benefit more fully from counseling because her thoughts and feelings had become stable enough to make proper use of the therapy. She was advised to take the medication on a regular basis regardless of how she felt and to continue taking it even if she felt like she no longer needed it. The doctor explained that in some cases, the medication could eventually be reduced or discontinued; more likely, however, the medication would need to be continued at a maintenance level. He explained that with rare exceptions, a cyclic mood disorder is a chronic condition that requires chronic treatment. The good news, however, was that the first-line mood stabilizers; namely, lithium and select anticonvulsants, are not addicting and could be taken long-term with minimal risk of side effects.

After nine months Sara discontinued psychotherapy but experienced a return of symptoms when she attempted to discontinue the Neurontin. Therefore, she resumed taking the medication with occasional follow-up visits with the psychiatrist.

EXPRESSION TWO
Bipolarity Disguised as Intrapsychic Conflict

Life is an emotional roller coaster. Happiness and sorrow; success and failure; victory and defeat; are a natural part of our daily lives. Under normal circumstances, our emotions correspond to the psychosocial situation in which we find ourselves. As discussed in chapter one, the internal workings of the soul interface with electrical circuits in the brain to create the various emotions that we experience each day.

However, in the case of a mood disorder, the limbic system of the brain is not functioning normally; inappropriate messages are being sent to the soul. This causes persons with mood disorders to experience emotions that are either exaggerated or inappropriate to the circumstances in which they find themselves. When the soul reacts to these emotions, it further stimulates neuronal circuits that are already overactive in mood disorders. As emotions escalate, intrapsychic and interpersonal tensions rise. Unaware of what is happening in their brains, individuals with mood disorders either blame themselves or others for the emotional tension they experience. The result is a viscous cycle in which neurologically generated emotions such as anxiety, irritability, anger, and depression are compounded by intrapsychic tensions that create the same emotions. In essence, the brain and the soul get into a metaphysical shouting match that can create one emotional crisis after another if left untreated.

In bipolar disorders, this phenomenon occurs intermittently, thus giving rise to symptoms that come and go. The intermittent nature of the symptoms creates another layer of confusion for the sufferer and tends to undermine all efforts to achieve consistency in social and occupational functioning. Each time the person with a cyclic mood disorder begins a project, makes a resolution, or attempts to modify a destructive behavior, he gets derailed. After repeated failures, he gradually loses confidence in his ability, in his choices, and in himself. The chronic emotional pain can lead to social withdrawal, substance abuse, sexual promiscuity, eating disorders, and other maladaptive behaviors that further obscure and compound the underlying abnormality. It can also cause a major depressive episode that is superimposed upon the cyclic mood disorder.

Most persons cannot tell what part of their emotional response is due to a brain abnormality and what part is due to their psychosocial environment. Hence, when patients with a mood disorder give the doctor their history, they tend to rationalize their thoughts, feelings, and behaviors around triggers to which they can relate. For example, a woman who seeks treatment for depression and insomnia might assume that her abusive husband is the cause of her difficulties. Therefore, she would be likely to present her symptoms in the context of her failing marriage. Similarly, a college student who seeks treatment for anxiety and poor concentration might attribute his symptoms to a heavy course load and the need to earn good grades. Hence, he would be likely to present his symptoms in the context of academic pressure. This kind of misattribution of symptoms can lead even experienced mental health professionals to the wrong conclusion about the root cause of the patient's symptoms. Consequently, many patients with mood disorders are mistakenly referred for psychotherapy under the assumption that the entire problem is situational.

Until this is more widely recognized, all efforts to help the average patient with a mood disorder will be undermined by the elusive abnormality in his brain. Not only will the mood disorder undermine his progress in therapy, but misattribution of symptoms can lead the therapist to revisit issues that the patient has long since resolved. Worse yet, discussing such issues can stimulate dysphoric circuits in the brain that are already hyperexcitable in mood disorders, thus worsening the depressive symptoms. Hence, mood disorders can actually be exacerbated by poorly timed and misdirected psychotherapy.

A safer and more expeditious approach is to search for and, if present, treat any underlying neurochemical abnormalities prior to or concurrent with intensive psychotherapy. This approach improves the efficacy of psychotherapy and maximizes the benefits. Attempting to treat electrochemical abnormalities of the brain with psychotherapy alone is like attempting to bail water out of a boat that has a hole in it—it might help for a while, but the symptoms will keep flooding back until the underlying neurochemical abnormality is treated.

The reverse problem can occur when psychotropic medication is prescribed for emotional problems that are entirely psychological.

Psychotropic medications are designed to correct electrochemical abnormalities of the brain, not to reduce the intrapsychic tension that is a normal part of life. Attempting to medicate intrapsychic pain is tantamount to using alcohol to mend a broken heart—it prevents the patient from growing emotionally and spiritually.

Therefore, determining the underlying cause of the patient's symptoms is essential to effective treatment. The key to distinguishing neurochemical causes of emotional pain from psychological causes is the degree to which the emotional responses seem appropriate to the psychosocial milieu. In the absence of a neurochemical abnormality, most individuals will react appropriately to everyday stressors. They will not repeatedly overreact, underreact, or oscillate between being appropriate one moment and inappropriate the next.

When the inconsistencies are striking, family members and significant others can be invaluable in helping the clinician rule in or rule out the diagnosis of a mood disorder. Then again, in cases where the inconsistencies are subtle, family members often rationalize the patient's behavior in the same way that the patient does. Under these circumstances, the clinician must take a meticulous history and ask pointed questions in order to accurately assess the psychological and biochemical constituents of the patient's symptoms. The following case illustrates the challenge of making an accurate diagnosis.

CLINICAL CASE VIGNETTE

Twenty-three-year-old female with severe anxiety and obsessive worries about her health

A twenty-three-year-old college student was working toward her nursing degree at a major university. As a child, she suffered from severe asthma and environmental allergies, which frequently caused her to miss school and had prevented her from participating in athletics. Her years of personal struggle with illness gave her a sense of compassion for the sick, and by the time she had graduated from high school, she had decided to pursue a career in nursing.

Although she was intrigued by anatomy, physiology, and many of her other classes, she started to become anxious as her studies became more clinically oriented. As she learned about diabetes, lupus, and other chronic diseases, she began to fear that she might have one of them. She had always been somewhat of an anxious person, but now her worries were beginning to interfere with her academic performance and enjoyment of learning.

Despite her attempts to reassure herself that she did not have any of the illnesses that she was studying, her worries drove her deeper and deeper into the study of them. Although this benefited her academically, it was causing her to worry more, rather than less. Over time, she worked herself into a vicious cycle of anxiety from which she could find no escape.

Out of desperation, she turned to food for comfort. At times, it seemed to help, but at other times, it compounded the problem because of her fear of gaining weight. Eventually, she found herself both anxious and overweight.

Unsure of what to do, she discussed the matter with one of her instructors. After hearing the problem, her pathology professor related a personal experience in which she, as a medical student, thought she had multiple sclerosis. She kindly took the time to share her story, as well as the happy ending. Although this gave Anna some relief, her worries soon returned. Over the following months, her grades began to deteriorate, and she started to have doubts about her choice of career. Not knowing where else to turn, she sought the help of a psychologist.

Treatment began with an exploration of Anna's past in relationship to her current problem. The therapist noted that Anna became visibly anxious as she described her frequent visits to the doctor and many hospitalizations for asthma as a child. Anna told the therapist that as she was growing up, her illness had interfered with everything in her life.

After only a few sessions, the therapist formulated the hypothesis that Anna's studies in the medical field were reawakening unresolved fears of vulnerability and loss of control that her asthma had created. Although the therapist's support and reassurance gave Anna a sense of hope, she continued to fear that she might be developing diabetes.

Approximately three months into therapy, Anna was hospitalized with a severe bout of asthma that had been triggered by an upper respiratory tract infection. Her worries about having diabetes were substantiated when laboratory tests showed a mild elevation of her glucose. Despite reassurance from the attending physician that the blood sugar elevation was more likely due to the stress of the infection than diabetes, Anna's anxiety reached an all-time high.

On the third hospital day, the medical team felt that Anna's anxiety was interfering with her progress, and so a psychiatric consultation was ordered. After a thorough assessment, the psychiatrist felt that Anna might benefit from an antidepressant and a tranquilizer. The doctor prescribed Prozac and Klonopin. He told Anna that the medications were intended to reduce her anxiety and lift her spirits but that the antidepressant might not reach full effect for several weeks.

Within days, Anna began to feel more at ease, but the medications were also causing her to feel a little "numb" emotionally. After her discharge from the hospital, she resumed psychotherapy and continued to take her medications. During the weeks that followed, Anna noticed that her anxiety was under better control but that there were still times when she felt very anxious and obsessed with worry. At her first follow-up visit with the psychiatrist, Anna's doctor increased the Prozac to 40mg per day.

After the dosage increase, Anna began to feel even more anxious. But before she could get back in to see the psychiatrist, she was notified of an insurance change and was forced to see a different psychiatrist. Her therapist recommended a colleague, who re-evaluated the case.

In addition to taking a thorough history, the new psychiatrist contacted Anna's parents to obtain collateral information. Anna's mother described her as anxious, shy, and insecure. She also described the enormous stress that Anna's asthma attacks had placed upon the whole family as she was growing up. Then, shortly after starting high school, Anna had become increasingly moody. When asked for more detail about this, both parents described inconsistencies in Anna's day-to-day functioning. They described her as having two sides: there was the quiet and shy Anna; and then there was the high energy, perfectionist Anna. This pattern had become more prominent around her sophomore year of high school and had at times interfered with her participation in family functions and her relationships with peers.

From the parents' perspective, the stress of college seemed to have been making their daughter even more anxious and moody. When asked about her current problem, Anna's parents worried that Anna's life-long struggle with asthma might have turned her into a hypochondriac. Thus, they questioned Anna's choice of career.

After reviewing all of the information, the doctor concluded that Anna was suffering not only from a reawakening of the emotional trauma created by her asthma but also from a cyclic mood disorder characterized by waves of anxiety that caused her to become terrified of illness as a result of repeated experiences in which the anxiety produced by her mood disorder was paired with anxiety-provoking physical symptoms and medical treatments as a child. Her quest to become a nurse was potentially therapeutic in that it was not only an opportunity to make a meaningful contribution to society, but it was also an opportunity to master the trauma of her illness.

The doctor's assessment also provided a possible explanation for the timing of Anna's symptoms. Cyclic mood disorders generally develop during late childhood and early adolescence, which was about the time that Anna's anxiety about her illness took a big jump. They also tend to be exacerbated by psychological and physical stress, which would help explain why Anna had become more symptomatic when her pre-nursing curriculum began to remind her of her own illness, and why her symptoms reached an all-time high when she developed the respiratory tract infection. At the time of her hospitalization, Anna was under the academic stress of her falling grades, the psychological and physical stress of her asthma and its recurrence, and the emotional stress of an exacerbation of her cyclic mood disorder, the latter being due not only to the first two factors but also to the high dose of antidepressant she was taking together with the stimulant medications that she was receiving to help her breathe. The doctor explained that the stimulant effects of antidepressants and bronchodilators could exacerbate the symptoms of a cyclic mood disorder, as could the steroids Anna was receiving.

The doctor who had started Anna on Prozac probably assumed that Anna's anxiety was part of a classic depression. However, the family history suggested that Anna had been having mood swings since early adolescence. Her rapid but unsustained response to the antidepressant was further evidence that she might have a cyclic mood disorder. The doctor explained that this scenario is common in patients with cyclic mood disorders that are misdiagnosed and treated with antidepressants.

Based upon the new diagnosis, the doctor recommended that Prozac be replaced with a mood stabilizer. Because anxiety was a prominent symptom, Neurontin was selected. Neurontin tends to be a good first choice when anxiety is a prominent component of a cyclic mood disorder. Like most of the mood stabilizers, Neurontin was initially marketed for the treatment of epilepsy; hence, it is more widely known as an "anticonvulsant."

After just two doses of Neurontin, Anna felt calmer and more collected. She was able to return to her studies and, because the effect of the medication was sustained, she gradually became less obsessed about her health. The observation that a medication could make such a big difference in such a short time began to convince Anna that her fear and anxiety were due more to an abnormality in her brain than to a fault of her own or the trauma of her past. This fresh perspective helped restore her hope and helped her stop blaming herself.

During the course of treatment, Anna learned more about her mood disorder. This helped her overcome her paralyzing fear of illness and allowed her to formulate a more positive and realistic self-image. Anna eventually graduated from nursing school and accepted a position as a psychiatric nurse.

EXPRESSION THREE
Bipolarity in Child Abuse and Neglect

Cyclic mood disorders are highly genetic. The relative risk of inheriting bipolar disorder (the most severe form of cyclic mood disorder) is seven times that of the general population. The risk of the disorder in a monozygotic twin of a person with bipolar disorder is approximately sixty times that of the general population. However, the actual risk of inheriting the disorder is probably even higher than indicated by these statistics because bipolar disorder is often misdiagnosed as major depressive disorder or dysthymia, and these cases are not included in the studies of genetic transmission. The problem of misdiagnosis is even greater for "soft forms" of bipolar disorder, which include bipolar II disorder, cyclothymia, cyclic depression, and depressive mixed states. Considering this, the numbers for genetic transmission of disorders in the bipolar spectrum are probably much higher than most studies report. Be that as it may, parents who have mood swings have a high risk of bearing children who have moods swings. Affected families have an elevated risk of domestic violence, abuse, and neglect. This is especially true when both parents have a mood disorder. In addition to having turbulent marriages, parents with mood disorders tend to be inconsistent in caring for and disciplining their children. When they are depressed, they are at risk for neglecting or abusing their children; when they are manic, they are at risk for overindulging them. Some affected persons have periods of abnormally high sexual arousal, which can increase tension in the marriage and lead to extramarital affairs. It can also lead to child sexual abuse, incest, and other sexually deviant behaviors.

Worse yet, the child who has inherited a cyclic mood disorder finds himself alternately overreacting and underreacting to stressors at home and at school. This inconsistency is not only disconcerting to the child but also undermines his ability to develop healthy coping mechanisms. As a result, his emotional development is stunted and his social and academic progress, delayed. Out of desperation, such children frequently resort to denial, repression, and other unhealthy coping mechanisms that further impede their emotional, intellectual, and spiritual growth. By the time they are adults, many of them have emotional wounds that are as difficult to sort out as they are to heal. This is especially true of those who have learned to distrust even those who offer to help them.

CLINICAL CASE VIGNETTE

Sixteen-year-old whose parents have undiagnosed cyclic mood disorders

Charlie lived in a household where his parents never seemed to stop arguing, and rules and expectations were always changing. Worse yet, Charlie was given little affirmation for his achievements; on the contrary, he was often blamed for things that were not his fault. As a result, he feared his parents and learned to blame himself for the disappointments in his life.

As Charlie grew older, his fear of his parents turned into hostility and lack of respect, and he became oppositional and defiant. He had become tired of being told what to do and wanted to do things his own way despite his doubts about himself. Meanwhile, Charlie's mother would seek emotional comfort from him after her arguments with his father. This added to Charlie's resentment toward his father and increased the shame he already felt for disrespecting his parents. By the age of thirteen, Charlie felt insecure, angry, and entitled. He would lose control whenever he could not have his way, sometimes lashing out at his parents verbally and physically.

In school, Charlie paid little attention and was frequently disruptive. He had already been enrolled in emotionally delayed (ED) classes, but rather than going to class, he would spend time with older boys who were either truant or had dropped out of school. He had also started smoking cigarettes, and his parents suspected that he was experimenting with marijuana.

Due to concerns about Charlie's truancy and poor academic performance, the school held a multidisciplinary conference and recommended home visits and weekly counseling sessions. A psychiatric evaluation was also recommended.

During the intake evaluation with a child and adolescent psychiatrist, Charlie initially demonstrated an attitude of indifference; but about half way through the interview, he turned angry and defiant. His sudden change in demeanor was seemingly unprovoked and prompted the psychiatrist to consider the possibility that Charlie had a cyclic mood disorder. To investigate this further, the doctor asked Charlie's parents if they had noticed any sudden changes in Charlie's mood or temperament. Charlie's mother initially denied that Charlie's mood was unpredictable. But after thinking more about it, she realized that she had become so accustomed to his unpredictability that it had become predictable; he had become predictably unpredictable. She recalled first noticing Charlie's sudden shifts in mood when he was about eleven years old, but she had attributed them to puberty.

When questioned about this in greater detail, Charlie's mother described changes in Charlie's mood from playful and funny to quiet and irritable. Though most of his anger outbursts occurred when he was confronted about something or could not have his way, some of them seemed unprovoked. When asked whether Charlie was ever agreeable, Charlie's mother said yes but that that too was unpredictable. In the doctor's mind, the unpredictability of Charlie's behavior was enough to substantiate his suspicion that Charlie had a cyclic mood disorder. In general, any inconsistency in temperament or behavior is suggestive of a neurochemical trigger of one's emotions rather than a purely psychological one.

Charlie's mother also expressed frustration about Charlie's refusal to go to sleep at night and his difficulty getting up for school in the morning. With regard to this, the doctor again probed for any inconsistencies. Initially, Charlie's mother reported the problem as constant except on weekends when Charlie wanted to play with his friends. But after giving it more thought, she recalled a few instances in which Charlie had popped out of bed in the morning even on a school day. The inconsistency provided additional support to the doctor's suspicion that Charlie had a cyclic mood disorder.

Charlie's father expressed concerns that his son might also have a drug problem. Charlie had already been smoking cigarettes, but more recently, his parents had found an empty beer can and some drug paraphernalia in Charlie's room.

When the doctor questioned Charlie privately about any drug use, Charlie admitted to using marijuana. He also admitted to drinking on occasion and experimenting with cocaine. When the doctor inquired about the effects of cocaine, Charlie said that it made him feel less depressed and more focused. Alcohol and marijuana made him feel calmer.

Upon further questioning, Charlie described having racing thoughts, nervousness, and irritability, which interfered with his ability to concentrate in school and fall asleep at night. He expressed anger toward his parents for being so critical of him and said that he wanted to get a job and move out rather than remain in school and continue living at home.

After reviewing the history, the doctor explained to the family that Charlie had both a biological and a psychological problem. Biologically, he was suffering from a cyclic mood disorder complicated by attention deficit disorder (ADD). The cyclic mood disorder was causing the emotional instability that the doctor had observed in the office and which Charlie's parents had observed at home. It was also causing Charlie to have difficulty falling asleep at night and difficulty getting up in the morning. The ADD was causing him to be impulsive and distractible, thus explaining the difficulties Charlie was having controlling his anger at home and his concentration at school.

Psychologically, Charlie was struggling with uncomfortable feelings toward his parents and doubts about his ability to become a responsible adult. Thus, Charlie was not only experiencing surges of emotion that stemmed from an abnormality in his brain but he was also experiencing intense frustration about the conflicts in his life. The neurochemical abnormality had been compounding dysfunctional family dynamics, thus causing deeply rooted and persistent confusion in Charlie's life. For Charlie, becoming a responsible adult was like trying to become an accomplished pianist with an out-of-tune piano and constant criticism for playing poorly.

THE MANY FACES OF BIPOLAR DISORDER

Worse yet, the ADD was limiting both his ability to concentrate and his ability to contain his anger, thus creating a vicious cycle of failure, criticism, and frustration.

Treatment would begin by starting Charlie on a mood stabilizer in an effort to normalize his brain function. This would be followed by the addition of a psychostimulant, the standard treatment for ADD. The doctor explained that the two neurochemical problems would have to be treated in sequence because psychostimulants can sometimes worsen the symptoms of a cyclic mood disorder. Psychostimulants can also reduce the effectiveness of a mood stabilizer, which in turn can interfere with the ability to assess the effectiveness of either medication because the symptoms of a cyclic mood disorder can mimic ADD.

Although the first several mood stabilizers were ineffective, the doctor eventually found one that normalized Charlie's mood. This helped reduce his anger outbursts and relieve his depression. Approximately two weeks later, Dexedrine (dextroamphetamine), a psychostimulant, was added for the treatment of ADD.

Charlie's parents were eventually treated, which in turn facilitated their progress in marital therapy. Simultaneously, Charlie continued in individual and family therapy. The fact that both of his parents were willing to be treated was reassuring to him and helped keep him engaged in treatment. At the same time, it gave his parents a fresh perspective on their marital difficulties and a renewed sense of hope about mending their relationship.

With the help of medication and psychotherapy, Charlie's parents gradually became more patient with each other and with Charlie. Over time, Charlie gradually regained respect for his parents and, having both the incentive and a newfound ability to control his behavior, Charlie gradually changed his ways. He eventually let go of his anger toward his parents and himself, which in turn reduced his feelings of shame and gradually allowed him to build self-esteem.

EXPRESSION FOUR

Bipolarity in Anorexia and Bulimia

We live in a society that is becoming increasingly conscious about appearance, health, and fitness. From billboards and television adds to magazine articles and self-help books, we are constantly reminded about how we aught to look and feel. Not surprisingly, the thing most talked about is weight because weight most obviously affects how we look and how we feel.

However, some persons take their concerns about weight too far. They begin to count calories and over-restrict what they eat, the early signs of a condition called *anorexia nervosa*. Others eat excessively and then purge their food, the signs of a condition called *bulimia nervosa*. To date, the assumption has been that anorexia and bulimia are behavioral problems that reflect one's attitude and self-image. However, clinical experience has shown that most persons who develop an eating disorder actually have a mood disorder at the root of their dysfunctional eating.

As discussed earlier, mood disorders are caused by dysfunctional circuits in the brain. In some individuals, these circuits appear to involve appetite and satiety. When overactive, they can produce a feeling of hunger even if the individual has eaten recently. Conversely, a shift in the locus of hyperexcitability can produce a feeling of satiety even if the individual has not eaten for a lengthy period of time. Hyperexcitable circuits can also produce strong cravings for specific foods, such as sweets, fats, and salts. Thus, neuronal hyperexcitability can cause one's appetite to turn on and off, but not necessarily in synchrony with the normal pattern of hunger and satiety that occurs from meal to meal. The duration of hunger or satiety could vary from hours to days to weeks and promote restrictive eating, binge eating, or both. Superimposed upon this are the emotional swings that occur due to the involvement of mood circuitry. The varied and often rapidly changing feelings that are produced tend to further promote abnormal eating habits in an effort to gain control over one's emotions.

Unfortunately, the possibility of an underlying mood disorder is often overlooked in patients with eating disorders; instead, treatment tends to be restricted to individual and group psychotherapy. This oversight can prevent the patient from achieving full recovery, because long-standing patterns of behavior are hard to change, especially when the underlying cause is left untreated.

Therefore, the possibility of a neurochemical abnormality should be ruled out in every patient who seeks treatment for an eating disorder. Factors that should raise the suspicion of a mood disorder include a personal or family history of mood or anxiety disorders, a history of substance abuse, onset of symptoms during late childhood or early adolescence, an on-off (cyclic) pattern of food cravings, and difficulty satisfying cravings.

CLINICAL CASE VIGNETTE

Eighteen-year-old female with bulimia nervosa, obsessive-compulsive disorder, and chronic depression

Brittany was in her second week of college when she went to the student health service with complaints of weakness and shortness of breath. Test results showed that her potassium level was dangerously low, and so she was admitted to the university hospital for further evaluation and treatment.

Although Brittany initially withheld information about her dietary habits, she later told staff that she had been using laxatives and diuretics to lose weight. She also admitted that she had been binging and purging, particularly during the preceding few months.

A psychiatry consultation was ordered to further evaluate Brittany's eating habits and attitude toward her weight and appearance. During the evaluation, Brittany told the doctor that her weight was extremely important to her. She had been raised in a family where a premium was placed on appearance, and the starting of college was a very important time in her life.

Brittany was the second born of three siblings, having an older sister and a younger brother. Her sister had been very popular in high school and had just been accepted to law school, having earned near-perfect grades at the same university where Brittany now found herself hospitalized. Brittany's parents idolized her sister, which greatly added to the pressure Brittany felt to succeed. Doubting that she had her sister's intelligence, Brittany focused on her appearance in an effort to gain acceptance.

Since the beginning of high school, Brittany had been becoming increasingly preoccupied with her makeup, her clothing, and, especially, her weight. She was shorter than most of her classmates and was picked on in grade school for being overweight, a memory that made her feel even more self-conscious about being short. However, by her mid teens, she had become very successful at moderating her weight, having been willing to do whatever it took to remain thin.

By the start of her junior year in high school, Brittany's efforts to control her weight had become an obsession. She had progressed from healthful eating and regular exercise to an alternating pattern of restrictive eating and overeating. Some days she would abstain from food to the point of weakness, and other days she would binge-eat and then either purge or spend hours in the gym to burn off the calories. Whenever she felt like she was losing control of her weight, she would become anxious and depressed. The emotional discomfort would cause her to binge, and then purge in an effort to rid herself of the calories. Once she felt better, she would find the motivation to go to the gym.

Without realizing it, Brittany had developed a rigid behavior pattern that was running her life. However, there was nothing she could do, for as much as weight gain made her feel anxious and depressed, weight loss made her feel happy and alive. By the end of her junior year in high school, Brittany's dieting and weight control had become more important to her than her grades or her career. The friends she chose, the magazines she red, and the food she ate all revolved around losing weight and feeling good.

During Brittany's senior year in high school, her mother expressed concerns about her obsessive behavior and scheduled her an appointment with a psychologist. Brittany was initially reluctant to go; but after her mother threatened to cancel her gym membership, Brittany agreed to see the psychologist.

Although her weekly therapy sessions provided education, guidance, and support, they did not lead to any significant change in Brittany's behavior; she continued to spend most of her time thinking about how to lose weight. By the time of high school graduation, she was not only binging and purging, but she was also using diuretics and laxatives.

The doctor at the hospital explained that Brittany's frequent vomiting, together with her abuse of diuretics and laxatives, had led to potassium depletion, which in turn was causing muscle weakness. The electrolyte imbalance was also placing Brittany at risk for digestive problems and cardiac arrhythmias. As for the eating disorder, the consulting psychiatrist called attention to the cyclic nature of Brittany's binging and asked whether she was aware of any correlation between her mood changes and her appetite. Brittany reiterated that the feelings of depression and self-loathing following her binges would make her want to purge, but she did not know what caused her to overeat. She could only say that she sometimes had an insatiable appetite. Her cravings for food would usually begin abruptly, sometimes even in the middle of the night, and would typically include cravings for sweets and fatty foods such as cookies, chocolate, and peanut butter. At times the drive was so strong that Brittany would eat half the jar of peanut butter with a spoon or drink pancake syrup straight out of the bottle. Although she felt excited in the process of doing this, she would feel disgusted afterward, and then she would purge.

The doctor asked Brittany to keep a log of her binges, her mood, and her overall functioning after her discharge from the hospital. What eventually became apparent was that Brittany's eating pattern was cyclically related to her mood changes. Her binging episodes would occur every three to four days and would be preceded by a period of high energy and restrictive eating. The binge would usually be associated with feelings of depression and sluggishness that would resolve after she would purge. The mood chart helped Brittany see that she really wasn't depressed all the time and that her appetite, like her energy and motivation, came in waves that lasted several days at a time rather than for short periods of time between meals, as occurs in a normal person. The doctor explained that this abnormal pattern was caused by cyclic electrochemical changes in the brain that were difficult for Brittany to control. This helped explain Brittany's inability to make progress in psychotherapy. The doctor said that the problem is very common and usually begins around adolescence. Treatment with medication was indicated due to the medical nature of the abnormality.

Though a little hesitant, Brittany agreed to try a mood stabilizer. After two weeks on the medication, she began to notice that she had less depression and less of a drive to binge. Her concentration improved and became more consistent, and she felt more in control of her emotions and her life. She was amazed that medication could make such a difference for something that she felt certain was purely a function of her attitude and volition.

Over time, Brittany began to realize that a neurochemical abnormality in her brain was causing cyclic mood changes that she had been misattributing to feelings about her weight and appearance. This growing awareness helped her rebuild her self-image and reassess her life in the context of a medical condition that she needed to respect and treat.

After three months in treatment, Brittany was also diagnosed with obsessive-compulsive disorder, a related but clinically distinct neurochemical abnormality. Normally, obsessive-compulsive disorder is treated with high-dose antidepressants, which can exacerbate symptoms of a cyclic mood disorder unless, as in Brittany's case, the condition is already being treated with a mood stabilizer. With the addition of an antidepressant, Brittany eventually gave up the rituals that wasted so much of her time and was able to keep up with her studies. Four years later, she graduated from college with a degree in kinesiology.

EXPRESSION FIVE
Bipolarity in Alcoholism and Substance Abuse

Clinical experience has shown that most persons who abuse alcohol and other drugs have an underlying psychiatric condition, most commonly, a cyclic mood disorder. Their mood instability not only leads them into drugs but also reinforces their use of drugs.

When normal daily emotional stress is magnified by neurochemically-generated emotional stress, life can become overwhelming. As a result, many individuals with a cyclic mood disorder begin to develop unhealthy coping mechanisms; one of these is the use of alcohol and other drugs.

As previously discussed, the electrical disturbance that underlies a cyclic mood disorder classically creates a variety of symptoms, such as anxiety, depression, and apathy that alternate with feelings of optimism, confidence, and excitement. Although someone who feels well would probably not like the mind-altering effects of a psychoactive substance, the person with a mood disorder finds these effects attractive because they deliver him from the uncomfortable feelings that he lives with. Stimulants, such as cocaine and amphetamines, are typically used to counteract electrochemically-mediated lows and to amplifying electrochemically-mediated highs. Sedatives, such as alcohol and marijuana, are typically used to come off a high or reduce severe anxiety. Not surprisingly, most persons who abuse drugs get started during their teens, which is when the symptoms of a cyclic mood disorder typically begin.

In order to understand drug abuse in persons with a cyclic mood disorder, one must consider the relief that the affected person feels when a few drinks with a friend or a few joints at a party magically alleviate a wave of paralyzing anxiety; or when a few hits of speed or a few lines of cocaine replace a cloud of depression with a ray of sunshine. Psychoactive substances such as cocaine, amphetamines, alcohol, and marijuana often provide temporary and sometimes dramatic relief from the uncomfortable feelings that cyclic mood disorders create.

Therefore, parents, teachers, employers, and friends of those who abuse alcohol and other drugs should think about why the user is drawn to these drugs, rather than just pass judgment and demand that they quit. The most realistic and effective approach is to start by considering that there could be something wrong and suggest a psychiatric evaluation. Unfortunately, the matter is rarely handled this way. Instead, the user is usually blamed and criticized for his drug habit. This adds insult to injury because most persons who abuse drugs already feel ashamed of their habit. Hence, when they are confronted, they typically become defensive and unreceptive to advice.

In order to be of help, we must understand that most persons who abuse drugs benefit from them in ways that normal persons do not. But all too often, the only ones who recognize this are those who share the same problem—their peers. Unfortunately, their friends are rarely in a position to help. Therefore, those of us who *can* help should engage an addict by beginning with the assumption that he or she has a good reason for using drugs. This makes the user feel understood and respected rather than ashamed and rejected. A non-judgmental approach also makes the user more willing to explore his or her reasons for using drugs, and seek treatment.

Another barrier to effective intervention is accuracy in diagnosis. When an addict presents for treatment, the assessment of an underlying mood or anxiety disorder is complicated by symptoms produced by the drug or drugs of abuse as well as by symptoms of drug withdrawal. Both the use of psychoactive substances and withdrawal from them can produce symptoms that mimic a cyclic mood disorder. For example, "uppers," such as cocaine and amphetamines, can produce symptoms that mimic mania; whereas, tranquilizers, such as alcohol and marijuana, can produce symptoms that mimic depression. During the withdrawal phase, the opposite tends to occur as the central nervous system rebounds from these substances, thus creating the same wave pattern that characterizes cyclic mood disorders. A common error in the assessment and treatment of substance abuse is to assume that the drug or drugs of abuse are the cause of the emotional disturbance, rather than the other way around. Drugs of abuse can also mask the symptoms of a cyclic mood disorder, thus causing the user to appear as though he is not using when he actually *is* using, and using when he actually is *not* using. Even if the user remains abstinent for an extended period of time, the underlying mood disorder can make him appear as though he is still using. Hence, accurate diagnosis requires a great deal of experience on the part of the doctor and a great deal of trust on the part of the patient and family.

Contrary to traditional thinking, most persons who abuse drugs would be able to cope with life if their brains were functioning normally. But having a neurochemical abnormality is tantamount to having a car that has a bad alternator or a computer that has a virus. Over time, the problem creates disappointment, anger, and frustration, negative emotions that both add to and exacerbate the symptoms of a cyclic mood disorder. The resulting intrapsychic stress causes the brain to function even more abnormally, thus leading to substance abuse, sexual promiscuity, binge-eating, gambling, theft, violence, and other behaviors that further stress the soul. To this is added the emotional pain of criticism and rejection by loved ones, which in turn further exacerbates the symptoms of a cyclic mood disorder. In my opinion, over eighty percent of those who abuse alcohol and other drugs suffer from an underlying cyclic mood disorder.

Nevertheless, those who abuse drugs are usually blamed for their problems and for their addiction. Those pointing the finger might even include peers and former addicts, including those in Alcoholics Anonymous, Narcotics Anonymous, and other groups who confuse the symptoms of the underlying mood disorder with the effects of the drug or drugs of abuse. This confusion has led some spokespersons, group leaders, and organization members to shun the use of psychotropic medication and to view it as a failure to confront "the real problem" and "work a good program."

What adds to the confusion is that many persons who do not have a mood disorder have the same psychosocial stressors as those who do have one. The use of alcohol and illicit drugs, through their effects on the brain, can temporarily relieve emotional distress whether or not there is an underlying mood disorder. The recovery of the former group without medical-psychiatric treatment leads some persons to mistakenly believe that all substance abusers simply need to work hard and give up their habit. While there is no doubt that this is enough for many, there are many more for whom it is not enough.

Therefore, every person who abuses drugs or alcohol should have a thorough psychiatric evaluation. If a neurochemical abnormality is suspected, treatment should begin by asking the patient to remain abstinent from drugs of abuse for a period of time long enough to permit an adequate trial of psychotropic medication. A brief period of abstinence has three therapeutic advantages: first, it is more realistic than asking the patient to commit to never using drugs again; second, it gives medication an opportunity to take effect; and third, it gives the patient the opportunity to make a close comparison between medically-tested remedies and his or her drug or drugs of abuse.

Some persons either cannot or will not completely stop using drugs until psychotropic medication takes effect. In such cases, a trial of medication is better than no trial at all. Some clinicians might disagree with this approach, arguing that an underlying mood disorder is difficult to diagnose while a person is actively abusing drugs. Although active substance abuse does complicate the clinical picture, experience has shown that most individuals who abuse drugs have an underlying neurochemical abnormality that they are self-medicating. Hence, in those cases where there has not been a period of abstinence, the percentage approach is to begin treating any suspected neurochemical abnormality in the hope that a reduction in symptoms will allow the patient to transition from street drugs, which are toxic, to prescriptions drugs, which are therapeutic. In the event that there is no underlying neurochemical abnormality, a brief course of medication is less disadvantageous than leaving without treatment a person who has a neurochemical abnormality. In addition to alleviating symptoms, there is increasing evidence that effective treatment of a mood disorder can prevent or slow the progression of the neurochemical abnormality over time.

CLINICAL CASE VIGNETTE

Twenty-one-year-old with cyclic depression, cocaine abuse, and violent behavior

A twenty-one-year-old man was court-ordered into chemical dependency treatment after several arrests for cocaine possession and disorderly conduct. After a lengthy course of treatment in individual and group psychotherapy for substance abuse, concern arose that he might also be suffering from a mood disorder. Therefore, a psychiatric evaluation was requested.

The evaluating psychiatrist learned that Sam's legal record was extensive, primarily involving altercations with peers, including a recent charge of aggravated battery. His behavioral problems had prevented him from graduating from high school, and, since leaving school, he had been earning money doing odd jobs and part-time work. He spent the rest of his time watching television or hanging out with friends.

In addition to his difficulties maintaining gainful employment, Sam had difficulties in his relationships with women. His anger alienated one girlfriend after another, which further diminished his already low self-esteem. When he felt lonely, he would smoke cocaine, which would give him a "rush"; when he felt nervous, he would smoke marijuana, which would make him feel "mellow."

His comment to the psychiatrist about the "rush" from cocaine led to a discussion about his mood. Through careful questioning, the psychiatrist identified a history of several different and sometimes mixed mood states. Sam described periods when he felt very anxious, alternating with periods when he felt relatively calm. At other times, he would experience a wave of energy and enthusiasm that was sometimes accompanied by a return of the anxiety. His high-energy states were often followed by a period of intense irritability, which created problems in his relationships and with the law. He described his use of marijuana and alcohol as efforts to keep his anxiety and anger under control.

With regard to his developmental history, Sam described a pattern of dysfunctional family relationships, including verbal and physical abuse by his father. Sam's father was a chronic alcoholic, whose mood was unpredictable. His mother was afraid of his father, thus explaining why she often failed to protect Sam from unfair treatment by his father. Sam also had a brother and a sister, both of whom were struggling emotionally.

Academically, Sam had performed poorly since childhood and at one point was tried on Ritalin (methylphenadate) for attention deficit hyperactivity disorder (ADHD). However, the medication made him feel like a "zombie," and so he stopped taking it.

During the evaluation, Sam was polite and mild-mannered, showing no signs of agitation or the behavior problems reflected in his criminal history. He also seemed to have a genuine interest in improving the quality of his life but was not necessarily willing to stop using drugs.

After reviewing the history, the psychiatrist concluded that Sam was likely suffering from a cyclic mood disorder characterized by waves of anxiety, depression, irritability, and euphoria that sometimes occurred independently and sometimes occurred simultaneously. This was explained to Sam, and his drug problem was viewed as self-medicating.

Although Sam did not argue with this, he was reluctant to take any psychotropic medication. He said he was afraid that the medication might make him feel numb, which would take away his creativity. The doctor explained that street drugs, such as marijuana and cocaine, cause the brain to function abnormally, which prevents one from being himself, whereas psychotropic medications, such as mood stabilizers and antidepressants, normalize brain function and thereby allow one to be himself.

Sam remained skeptical. He countered with the argument that street drugs made him feel happy and productive, and what could be wrong with that? The doctor explained that such "highs" were artificial; that is, they are produced by abnormal, drug-induced, neurochemical changes in the brain rather than core beliefs and attitudes that constitute the character of a human being. In contrast, psychotropic medications normalize brain function, which allows one to develop as a person and discover his or her true self.

Still skeptical, Sam argued that he did not want to be dependent upon a drug for his emotional well-being. At that, the doctor pointed out that Sam was already dependent upon drugs—drugs that were toxic to the brain and the body. Nevertheless, Sam remained unwilling to take any medication. However, he did agree to schedule a follow-up appointment with the doctor.

Sam subsequently began seeing the doctor on a regular basis and eventually developed enough trust and respect for the doctor to try medication. At the initiation of therapy, Sam agreed to stop using all street drugs for one week, time enough for a mood stabilizer to take effect. With that, a small dose of Trileptal (oxcarbazepine) was started.

Sam returned to the doctor's office one week later with a new attitude toward treatment. He was amazed by how much the medication had reduced his depression and irritability, even after just two or three doses. The medication was gradually titrated to optimal effect, and Sam remained abstinent from street drugs with the exception of marijuana, which he continued to use because of persistent anxiety. The doctor explained that a single mood stabilizer, even when effective, was often insufficient to alleviate all the symptoms because the brain has many mechanisms for the production of symptoms. In an effort to reduce Sam's anxiety, Neurontin was added to the Trileptal, and Sam was asked to temporarily stop using marijuana. One week later, Sam retuned to the doctor's office amazed by the reduction in his anxiety. The medication was further adjusted to optimal effect, and Sam eventually gave up marijuana completely. At a subsequent office visit, Sam told the doctor that his improvement was so dramatic that it convinced one of his friends to stop using drugs and seek treatment.

EXPRESSION SIX
Bipolarity and other Addictive Behaviors

Because persons with cyclic mood disorders have overactive brain circuitry, they tend to be overly sensitive and excitable. While this might allow them to "feel" more deeply, it also increases their inclination to overindulge in emotionally stimulating behaviors. For example, the average person might be able to enjoy a day at the racetrack or a night at a casino without becoming addicted to gambling. But for the person with hyperexcitable neurons, the "rush" associated with gambling and other emotionally charged behaviors can be especially intense and, consequently, highly addictive. Hence, persons with cyclic mood disorders are at increased risk for developing addictions to gambling, drugs, sex, and other behaviors that create emotional excitement.

CLINICAL CASE VIGNETTE
Eighteen-year-old with substance abuse and pathological gambling

Steven was the youngest of eleven siblings. He grew up in a chaotic household and was raised primarily by his older siblings because both of his parents worked long hours. By the age of ten, he was hanging out in bars and pool halls, where he was introduced to the game of billiards. Steven took an immediate liking to the game and soon became highly proficient. He especially enjoyed the thrill of running the table and of taking money from his opponent. By the age of sixteen, he had dropped out of high school and was spending all his time gambling at the pool table.

On numerous occasions, his parents confronted him about his drinking and idleness, but it was no use; he would only become defensive and fly off the handle. The matter came to a head one evening when Steven got into an argument with a man he was hustling at the pool table. The altercation became physical, and Steven was stabbed with a knife. The owner of the establishment called an ambulance, and Steven was taken to the hospital. When he arrived at the emergency room, he started shouting at staff and making threats against the man who stabbed him. He was placed in restraints, and, while he was being treated medically, a psychiatric consultation was ordered to assess his risk of harming himself or others.

Steven boisterously told the consulting psychiatrist that the man who had stabbed him had refused to pay on the bet he had lost and had made a pass at his girlfriend. After meeting with Steven briefly, the psychiatrist decided to postpone the full assessment until Steven was no longer intoxicated.

Several hours later, Steven had calmed down enough to cooperate with the doctor. He admitted to using alcohol and other drugs and abandoned his threats to hurt anyone. He went on to talk about his gambling, which included billiards, poker, and sports betting. When asked how he had started gambling, he said he enjoyed playing pool and thrived on the excitement of winning money. When asked about his use of drugs, he said that alcohol helped him remain calm at the pool table. He later found that marijuana had a similar effect. Cocaine and other stimulants gave him an emotional high.

He denied any history of depression but admitted to having a hot temper. He boasted about his success at gambling and all the money he had won. He described his energy as "good" but said that he would periodically sleep for a few days in a row. His diet included caffeinated coffee and soda, which he said gave him an energy boost.

When collateral history was obtained from Steven's parents, he was described as nervous and moody. His girlfriend said that his emotions were unpredictable and his temper, volatile. At times, however, he could be easygoing and funny. That was the Steven that everyone liked.

The doctor concluded that Steven had a cyclic mood disorder. The cycling of his energy, the unpredictability of his temper, and the robustness of his response to caffeine and other stimulants were characteristic of bipolar spectrum disorder. The doctor explained that the disorder usually develops during early adolescence. This comment caught the attention of Steven's parents, who recalled the abrupt change in Steven's behavior shortly after starting high school. As a child, he had been polite, obedient, and hard working; but around the age of thirteen, he had turned moody, oppositional, and idle, spending most of his time hanging out with a group of delinquent peers rather than his old friends, who had been a much better influence on him.

The doctor told Steven's parents that the sudden shift in Steven's temperament and behavior was typical of teens who develop a cyclic mood disorder. He said that early and aggressive treatment was of critical importance in preventing secondary and often more difficult problems, such as low self-esteem, truancy, and legal problems. This having been said, the doctor recommended that Steven begin taking the mood stabilizer Trileptal. The goal was to remove the precipitant of Steven's problems by correcting the abnormality in his brain.

At his first follow-up visit, Steven told the doctor that the medication did not seem to make any difference. Therefore, Trileptal was discontinued, and Neurontin was started. After just two days on Neurontin, Steven became calm and pleasant. He stopped losing his temper and became more patient. His girlfriend accompanied him to his second follow-up visit and told the doctor that Steven had become the person that she had fallen in love with when they first started dating. Steven reported feeling calmer and more focused; he also felt as though others were treating him better. As he continued taking the medication and seeing the doctor for psychotherapy, he began to think more about his future and increased his involvement in academic and family functions. His relationship with his girlfriend continued to improve, and they eventually got married.

EXPRESSION SEVEN
Bipolarity in Postpartum Depression

Postpartum depression is defined as a depressive episode that begins during the first month following labor and delivery. However, when a careful history is taken in women with postpartum depression, the majority of them report having had waves of mild depression, anxiety, or racing thoughts that either diminished or completely subsided during pregnancy, only to return with greater intensity after giving birth. The cyclic nature of these symptoms both prior to and after pregnancy suggests that many cases of postpartum depression might actually be postpartum exacerbations of an undiagnosed cyclic mood disorder. If this were so, we would expect to see not only depressive syndromes but also various other symptoms of bipolarity during the postpartum period, such as anxiety, irritability, hypomania, and mania. Indeed, this is what has been observed and has been reported in the literature. And in women with a pre-pregnancy diagnosis of bipolar disorder, the onset of depression, mania, or hypomania during the postpartum period is common.

The neurochemical basis of the remission of depressive symptoms during pregnancy is unclear but could involve a neuronal membrane stabilizing effect of elevated progesterone levels during pregnancy. After the baby is born and progesterone levels return to baseline, rebound neuronal membrane hyperexcitability would tend to create the postpartum emotional instability that characterizes postpartum depression. This phenomenon would also explain why bipolar disorder and cyclothymia, conditions that are presumably due to neuronal hyperexcitability, tend to become exacerbated during the postpartum period. Beyond that, the similarity of these conditions to premenstrual syndrome (PMS) suggests that postpartum mood disorders might actually be a kind of postpartum PMS that, like monthly PMS, is associated with a rapid fall in progesterone levels.

Unaware that her emotional system is being affected by the physiological changes of pregnancy, the expectant mother tends to rationalize her feelings. She might assume that her sense of well-being during pregnancy is due purely to her excitement about the baby. If such feelings become increasingly amplified during the postpartum period, as in postpartum mania, that too could be rationalized, at least in its early stages. Conversely, depressive symptoms like self-doubt, nervousness, and irritability could just as easily be rationalized, particularly if the baby is the woman's first, and the bulk of the responsibility for caring for the baby is hers.

Because the symptoms of a cyclic mood disorder tend to be exacerbated during the postpartum period, postpartum depression or mania is, for many women, the first sign of bipolarity. In all suspected cases, a thorough psychiatric evaluation should be obtained in order to clarify the diagnosis and weigh out the potential advantages and disadvantages of taking medication.

In addition to understanding the needs and benefits of treatment, there are several reasons that the characteristics and clinical course of bipolarity in women of childbearing age is important to understand. First, in light of the mood-stabilizing effect of pregnancy, many women who are taking medication for bipolar spectrum disorder might be able to reduce or discontinue the medication as part of pre-pregnancy planning. Even if symptoms were to return during the pregnancy, the first trimester, which is the high-risk period for medication-induced fetal malformations, might be completed or nearly completed. Restarting medication during the second or third trimester is much safer because the major organs of the body have already formed by that time. Second, the tendency for symptoms to re-emerge with increased severity during the postpartum period underscores the importance of restarting pre-pregnancy psychotropic medications immediately following labor and delivery. Those who restart their medications should consider alternatives to breastfeeding because most psychotropic medications pass into the breast milk, and their effects on the infant are not fully understood. Although there are many benefits to breastfeeding, the emotional wellness that effective psychotropic medication confers to the mother is worth the sacrifice, particularly in the United States and other developed countries, where a wide variety of highly nutritious infant formulas are available. Third, a diagnosis of postpartum depression after the first pregnancy signals the possibility that postpartum depressive symptoms are part of a condition that was previously sub-clinical and which, if properly treated, could bring the patient to a higher level of functioning than before she had become pregnant. Additionally, finding an effective medication can facilitate immediate symptom relief in the event that symptoms re-emerge during or after a future pregnancy or at another time in a woman's life. As with most illnesses, finding a medication that is effective for a mood disorder often requires several medication trials. Ideally these trials should be performed at a time when symptoms are mild, rather than when they are more severe or emerge during pregnancy. Fourth, the emergence of postpartum depressive symptoms is suggestive of an underlying bipolar-type disorder. This is important to recognize in light of the destabilizing effects that an antidepressant can have on a cyclic mood disorder that has been misdiagnosed as unipolar depression. As previously discussed, a mother's neurochemical system is already on the rebound during the postpartum period, and mismanagement of depressive symptoms with an antidepressant carries the risk of further destabilizing mood. Exacerbating depressive or manic symptoms during the postpartum period is potentially dangerous to the mother, her children, and her marriage, considering the potential for bipolar symptoms to result in inattentiveness, child neglect, domestic violence, and extramarital affairs. Therefore, a woman's pre-pregnancy, pregnancy, and postpartum emotional functioning should be carefully assessed before prescribing an antidepressant. If there have been previous pregnancies, the emotional symptom pattern before and after those pregnancies should be thoroughly explored. If there were any doubt about the diagnosis, initiating treatment with an anticonvulsant followed by reassessment would be safer than reflexively starting antidepressant therapy.

CLINICAL CASE VIGNETTE

Twenty-three-year-old female with postpartum depression

A twenty-three-year-old woman began to feel anxious two weeks after giving birth to her first child. Her anxiety centered upon fears that she was not caring for her newborn properly and that she might not be a good mother. As time went on, she also began to have difficulty sleeping and, to her horror, she began to have intrusive thoughts of physically harming her baby. The whole thing took her by surprise, because she had spent the entire pregnancy looking forward to the day when her baby would be laid in her arms. Now she felt trapped between the responsibility of caring for her child and telling her husband the awful things she was thinking and feeling.

Over the next several weeks, her anxiety continued to escalate and eventually reached the point where she was barely able to function. She cautiously began to relate hints of the problem to her husband, but he downplayed it all and tried to reassure her. He suggested that she ask her mother for support and help with the baby.

At first, this seemed like a good idea; but Linda soon found that her mother's help and reassurance provided only temporary relief. The moment she was alone again, all her fears and anxieties returned, and her insomnia left her feeling more exhausted each day.

The whole nightmare came to a head when Linda experienced a panic attack while driving to her mother's house. While on the highway with her infant in the back seat, she suddenly began to feel like she was suffocating and feared that she might lose control of the car. With her heart pounding like it was going to jump out of her chest, she quickly pulled to the side of the road, nearly sideswiping the car next to her. Somehow, she was able to bring the car to a safe stop, where she continued to experience what she thought was a heart attack. Moments later, a policeman pulled up behind her and called for an ambulance.

In the emergency room, Linda was given oxygen by mask and asked detailed questions about what brought her to the hospital. After an electrocardiogram was performed and blood work was taken, she was given a tranquilizer. She began to calm down after she was told that her test results were normal. After further review, the attending physician concluded that Linda had had a panic attack. She was discharged from the hospital with a small prescription for Ativan (lorazepam) and a psychiatric referral.

Although hesitant to follow-up, Linda eventually made an appointment with a psychiatrist. At the intake evaluation, she was asked about her current symptoms as well as her functioning during and prior to her pregnancy. From the history, the doctor identified a pattern of intermittent anxiety and depression that had actually been present since adolescence but which had become much more pronounced after Linda returned home from the hospital with her baby. The doctor was not surprised by Linda's relative wellness during her pregnancy and explained that cyclic mood changes commonly remit during pregnancy, only to return with greater intensity after delivery.

The doctor's understanding and compassion won Linda's trust and enabled her to divulge her deepest and most frightening secret—the fact that she had been having thoughts of harming her baby. To Linda's surprise, the doctor was not judgmental or overly alarmed; instead, he calmly provided reassurance and a medical explanation for what was happening. He explained that such thoughts were miss-firings of the brain—"electrical storms," he called them—that she should try to ignore until the problem could be treated. He said that the panic attack was a related but different phenomenon. The solution, he said, was to first calm the brain with an anticonvulsant (mood stabilizer), and then prevent future panic attacks with either a low dosage of antidepressant or an anti-anxiety medication or both if necessary.

The doctor explained that there were over ten different mood stabilizers available, each having an approximate thirty percent chance of working. Thus, he prepared Linda for the possibility that she might need to try several different medications before an effective one could be found. The doctor also warned that some of the mood stabilizers might be only partially effective and that two or more of them might need to be combined in order to completely eliminate her symptoms.

In light of Linda's difficulty sleeping and her need to hear the baby at night, the doctor prescribed Keppra. He explained that for most patients, Keppra was non-sedating yet had the potential of calming Linda's brain enough to allow her to fall asleep naturally. Linda was to increase the dosage gradually until she either felt better or experienced side effects.

With the first dose of 125mg, she slept better but experienced only a partial improvement in her daytime nervousness and worry. As the dosage was increased, Linda began to feel more tired during the day, and so the medication was reduced back down to 125mg each night. At this point, the doctor recommended adding a second mood stabilizer, Neurontin. The Neurontin was initiated at 100mg twice per day, and then increased to three times per day.

The effect was subtle but immediate. After only two doses, Linda began to feel calmer and more self-assured. The medication was subsequently increased to 200mg thrice daily. By the end of the first week on Keppra and Neurontin, Linda was sleeping normally again, and she was beginning to care for her baby the way she had envisioned while she was pregnant. She also noticed that the horrifying thoughts of hurting her baby had disappeared.

During the fourth week of treatment, Linda had another panic attack, though not as severe as the one that sent her to the emergency room. The doctor addressed this by starting her on a low dose of the antidepressant Zoloft (sertraline). Linda was to start the medication at 25mg per day and increase the dosage only if her panic attacks did not resolve within two weeks. Zoloft was effective in eliminating Linda's panic attacks, and it noticeably improved her mood.

Due to concerns about the medication passing into her breast milk, Linda elected not to breastfeed. But it was a small sacrifice for the relief that she was receiving from the medications and the loving care that her baby was receiving from a happier mom.

After approximately six months, the doctor suggested that Linda try to reduce her medication. He recommended that she discontinue Zoloft first because antidepressants have stimulant effects that, while potentially reducing symptoms of anxiety and depression, can also increase mood cycling. In order to reduce the risk of serotonin withdrawal symptoms, the Zoloft was gradually reduced and then discontinued without any withdrawal effects or return of symptoms. Nonetheless, the doctor explained that panic attacks occur intermittently and could return after several months off antidepressant medication. Meanwhile, Neurontin had been shown to have a protective effect against anxiety. Therefore, the doctor recommended that Neurontin be continued until Linda remained anxiety-free for several months.

Unlike antidepressants, anticonvulsants can be discontinued abruptly without withdrawal symptoms (unless the patient has a seizure disorder). Therefore, when the time was right, Neurontin was simply discontinued. Within a few days, however, Linda started to notice a partial return of her symptoms, and so she elected to restart the medication.

Eighteen months later, Linda and her husband decided to have a second child. Due to the risk of birth defects when anticonvulsants are taken during pregnancy, the doctor recommended that Linda discontinue both the Keppra and the Neurontin. He also reminded her that her first pregnancy had stabilized her mood and that she would probably experience the same relief of symptoms with her second pregnancy. In the event that she were to have a reemergence of symptoms, she could opt to restart her medication, depending upon the severity of her symptoms and how far along she was in the pregnancy, bearing in mind that the high-risk period for most anticonvulsant-induced birth defects is in the first trimester. Thanks to her previous treatment, Linda had the added advantage of knowing which medications were effective for her, thus eliminating the need to experiment during her pregnancy.

The question of whether to continue any medication during pregnancy is complex and should take into consideration the type of medication, the potential benefit to the mother, the potential risk to the fetus, and the stage of pregnancy at which the medication is to be administered. In the case of psychotropic medications, which can have a profound effect upon the mother's thinking and behavior, the use of medication during pregnancy can be crucial not only to the health but sometimes even to the life of both mother and baby.

EXPRESSION EIGHT
Bipolarity and Co-morbid Physical Disorders

Patients with cyclic mood disorders commonly also suffer from migraine headaches, fibromyalgia, and/or irritable bowel syndrome. Although there are no definitive data pointing to a common pathophysiology for these disorders, their high rate of co-morbidity, their cyclic nature, and their response to treatment suggests that they might be different manifestations of the same abnormality.

Migraine is a recurrent form of headache characterized by unilateral (one-sided) onset, severe pain, nausea, and other neurological symptoms that are thought to be related to vascular changes inside and outside the skull. The cause of these vascular changes is unknown but could involve a cyclic electrochemical abnormality in the brain. Common forms of treatment include vasomodulators, narcotic analgesics, anticonvulsants, and antidepressants.

Fibromyalgia is a form of nonarticular rheumatism that is characterized by musculoskeletal pain, stiffness, spasms, fatigue, and sleep disturbance. The pathophysiology of the disorder remains unclear but might include abnormalities of the central and peripheral nervous system. Common forms of treatment include physical therapy, nonsteroidal anti-inflammatory drugs, muscle relaxants, and antidepressants.

Irritable bowel syndrome is characterized by an abnormal increase in the motility of the gastrointestinal tract that results in diarrhea and occasional pain in the lower abdomen. As with migraine and fibromyalgia, the pathophysiology of irritable bowel syndrome remains unclear but is thought to involve a more central neurochemical abnormality. Common forms of treatment include increasing dietary fiber, antidiarrheal drugs, minor tranquilizers, and antidepressants.

Although the pathophysiology of all the aforementioned syndromes remains unclear, all share several characteristics. All three syndromes commonly occur in the same person, flare up intermittently, are aggravated by emotional stress, and are treated with antidepressants. Those who suffer from these syndromes also tend to have cyclic changes in mood, energy, and motivation, an observation that leads to the possibility that the same neurochemical abnormality that underlies cyclic mood disorders is also involved in migraine headaches, fibromyalgia, and irritable bowel syndrome. Some clinicians believe that chronic low-grade inflammation of the bowel and imbalances in bowel flora might actually be the cause of many medical conditions that involve functional abnormalities in nervous tissue, including irritable bowel syndrome, migraine headaches, fibromyalgia, depression, bipolar disorder, schizophrenia, obsessive-compulsive disorder, autism spectrum disorders, and a host of other chronic illnesses. The observation that the associated abnormalities of bowel flora and ecology are correctable by healthy changes in diet makes the so-called "gut and psychology syndrome" a potentially promising area of research and intervention..

CLINICAL CASE VIGNETTE

Sixty-nine-year-old woman with recurrent headaches, mood swings, and prescription drug abuse

A sixty-nine-year-old mother of four children became severely depressed after her husband's unexpected death. He had been in fairly good health when he became dizzy while coughing and lost consciousness. Paramedics were called to the home and the man was rushed to the hospital, where he was diagnosed with a ruptured abdominal aortic aneurysm. He expired in surgery a few hours later.

When his wife was told, she sat motionless for some time before being taken home by family members. During the next several months, she became increasingly depressed and withdrawn. She began to spend increasing amounts of time in bed, a pattern that eventually progressed to the point where she would get up only to use the bathroom or to sift through pictures and letters that, if only temporarily, took her back to the happy times she shared with her husband.

Out of concern, her two daughters eventually contacted her internist, who prescribed an antidepressant. Despite increasing doses of the medication, there was little improvement in Cally's depressive symptoms. The problem was subsequently compounded when she returned to her old habit of drinking. Although Cally's alcohol intake was modest at first, she eventually progressed to the point where she was passing out. On one occasion, she failed to answer repeated telephone calls from her daughter. When her daughter went to the home, she found Cally heavily intoxicated, with food burning on the stove. A decision was finally made to take Cally to the hospital.

While being detoxified, Cally began to complain of pain in her legs, back, and abdomen. When these complaints were evaluated, the attending physician learned that Cally's physical symptoms were chronic and had been treated with pain medication for many years. When asked about her use of narcotics, Cally explained that nothing else was effective for her pain.

Given Cally's history of alcoholism and chronic pain of uncertain origin, the treatment team had concerns that Cally might have been abusing prescription pain medication. In an effort to evaluate this further, a chemical dependency consultation was ordered.

After reviewing the history, the consultant formulated Cally's problem as one of alcohol and prescription drug dependence that was now complicated by acute grief over the loss of her husband. The consultant recommended that Cally be confronted about her chemical dependency, have her pain medication reduced, and receive psychiatric follow-up.

Although Cally did not suffer any significant alcohol withdrawal symptoms while in the hospital, her complaints of pain increased and she developed a severe headache. When she became insistent upon needing additional pain medication, she was again confronted about her chemical dependency and asked whether she thought she might be using the medication to cope with her grief. She said that she did not know but that her back was aching and that her head was pounding. A neurology consult was ordered, and Cally was diagnosed with mixed tension and migraine headaches. The neurologist ordered an injection of non-narcotic pain medication, but Cally's pain remained intolerable. Because the team felt uncomfortable increasing the dosage of narcotic pain medication, a psychiatric consultation was ordered.

The psychiatrist took a detailed history, which included collateral information from family members. He also contacted the patient's primary care physician regarding her past use of pain medication. Her physician said that he had tried Cally on several different antidepressants over the years but that the only medication that brought her consistent relief was narcotic pain medication.

The patient's daughter described her mother's baseline functioning as very emotional and preoccupied with her physical health. When asked if her mother was moody, the daughter said that her mother had a tendency to overreact to things. When asked for more detail about this, the daughter described her mother as "an emotional rollercoaster." One day she was up, the next day she was down; but since the death of her husband, she had been consistently down.

When the patient was questioned further about her symptoms, it became apparent that the physical pain that had plagued her over the years was intermittent, usually occurring in relationship to emotional stress. Despite the effectiveness of her pain medication, Cally said that she disliked having to take it because it caused constipation, which added to her bowel problems.

After the assessment, the psychiatrist contacted the attending physician to discuss his treatment recommendations. He expressed the opinion that Cally was suffering from a cyclic mood disorder that had been exacerbated by the recent loss of her husband. Her life-long pattern of highs and lows had been converted to cyclic depression (depressive-range cycling) when she began to grieve the loss of her husband. The stress was also exacerbating her migraine headaches, fibromyalgia, and irritable bowel—all syndromes that are common in patients with cyclic mood disorders—and which tend to be exacerbated by the same stressors that cause anxiety and depression. Based upon that assessment, the psychiatrist recommended a mood stabilizer.

In discussing his recommendations with the patient, the psychiatrist reassured her that he believed that her physical pain was real and that the treatment team should address it as such. At the same time, he expressed the hope that a mood stabilizer would reduce some of her physical pain as well as her emotional pain.

With the patient's consent, Neurontin was started at a dosage of 200mg three times daily. After two doses, Cally experienced a slight calming effect, but nothing more. The following day, the dosage was increased to 300mg thrice daily. By the third day on the medication,

Cally was calmer and more cooperative, but she remained very depressed. The psychiatrist explained the difference between intrapsychic emotional pain and neurochemical emotional pain. The former, he said, is produced by the stress in our lives and is under the control of our will; the latter is produced by abnormal electrical activity in the brain and is not fully under our control.

The doctor felt that Cally was suffering from both forms of emotional pain. The loss of her husband was naturally causing her to grieve, but her grief was compounded by an abnormality in her brain that had been present since her teens. The psychiatrist recommended that both forms of emotional pain be treated, and he offered to see the patient for medication and psychotherapy following her discharge from the hospital.

Over the next eighteen months, Cally worked through her grief and tried several different mood stabilizers before settling on a combination of Neurontin, Trileptal, and Depakote (divalproex sodium). The combination of Neurontin and Trileptal worked well to normalize Cally's mood, and Depakote markedly reduced the frequency of her migraine headaches. This enabled Cally to take on some part-time work, which the doctor said would help her recover by keeping her mind active. After three years of treatment, Cally was feeling better than she had felt before she lost her husband.

EXPRESSION NINE
Bipolarity in Borderline and Dissociative Disorders

Historically, borderline states have represented a spectrum of disorders. However, borderline personality disorder has become more narrowly defined as a pervasive pattern of instability in interpersonal relationships, self-image, and affects that develops at an early age and manifests itself in identity disturbance, fears of abandonment, impulsivity, emotional turbulence, feelings of emptiness, transient psychotic symptoms, and recurrent suicidal behavior. Although the cause of borderline personality disorder is believed to be multifactorial, the extreme sensitivity and emotional lability of these persons suggests that they have hyperexcitable neurons and that the presence of such an abnormality might be important in the genesis of the disorder.

As discussed earlier, adolescents with bipolar spectrum disorder appear to develop soft signs of the disorder at an early age. Like borderline personality disorder, bipolar spectrum disorder is characterized by turbulence in relationships, social withdrawal, and the development of unhealthy coping mechanisms. The earlier the onset of bipolar symptoms, the more primitive and maladaptive the person's coping mechanisms are likely to be, especially if they are formed under the emotional stress that often exists in families who carry genes for bipolar spectrum disorder. The large overlap between the symptoms of borderline personality disorder and bipolar spectrum disorder raises the possibility that some patients with borderline personality disorder are either misdiagnosed or have an underlying cyclic mood disorder. Considering this, every patient who is diagnosed with borderline personality disorder should be considered for a trial of mood stabilizers.

The same reasoning would apply to dissociative disorders, which may be a developmental variant of borderline personality disorder. Under the same kinds of early life stressors as those who develop borderline personality disorder, persons with dissociative disorders develop an effective, though ultimately dysfunctional coping mechanism called *dissociation*. Dissociation is an extreme form of repression in which a person splits off aspects of the psyche for various periods of time, usually to avoid very painful emotional and physical experiences. In a minority of cases, dissociation occurs so frequently and for such long periods that multiple ego states develop and mature, thus giving rise to multiple personality disorder.

As with borderline personality disorder, clinical experience suggests that neuronal membrane hyperexcitability could play an important role in the development of dissociative disorders. The neuronal hyperexcitability in persons with cyclic mood disorders tends to magnify even mild emotional stressors. The development of multiple ego states (to defend against painful emotions) in multiple personality disorder and the extensive use of primitive defense mechanisms in the entire spectrum of dissociative disorders suggest that these illnesses could be driven, at least in part, by an underlying cyclic mood disorder. In my opinion, every patient who is diagnosed with a dissociative disorder should be considered for treatment with mood stabilizers as an adjunct to psychotherapy.

CLINICAL CASE VIGNETTE

Thirty-four-year-old woman with multiple personality disorder

Samantha grew up in a large family in rural Alabama. She was the oldest of five children, having four brothers and one sister. Her father was an abusive alcoholic who would come home drunk, hollering at her mother from the moment he walked in the door. Samantha would shudder as she listened to her father's loud voice and vulgar language berating her mother. The hollering would usually stay downstairs but would sometimes follow mommy up to her room. It was the upstairs yelling that frightened Samantha the most because it was then that her father would sometimes burst into her room and beat her with his belt for what he called "ease dropping."

One summer night the fighting started while Samantha was in her room playing with her bird, Freddy. In an effort to avoid "ease dropping" and to pretend that nothing was wrong, Samantha just kept talking to her bird. The weather was stormy that night, and the thunder was scary, so Samantha tried to pretend that it was daytime and that the sun were about to make a beautiful rainbow.

Just as Samantha began to tell Freddy about the pot of gold at the end of the rainbow, her father stormed into the room and began to unfasten his belt. The thunder of his voice caused Freddy to leap off Samantha's finger and fly up to the ceiling. Dreading what was going to happen next, Samantha fantasized that she too could fly, and so she joined Freddy in the air. Things were not so painful this time, for Samantha's mind had gone elsewhere; she was safe with Freddy.

From that day forward, Samantha established the routine of talking to Freddy and flying away with him whenever her father would come home hollering. Samantha promised Freddy that she would never leave him and that she would always protect him from her father.

During her late teens, Samantha started dating a young man, but before long the relationship turned stormy. One of the things that really frustrated her boyfriend was Samantha's poor memory. She would lose blocks of time, which really angered him. Eventually, he insisted that she see a doctor.

Upon assessment by her primary care physician, Samantha was identified as having symptoms of depression and anxiety. She was referred to a psychiatrist, who determined that Samantha also had a dissociative disorder. The psychiatrist started her on an antidepressant and referred her to a colleague for psychotherapy.

After reviewing the recent history, the therapist explored Samantha's family life, with special attention to her history of abuse as a child. Initially, Samantha felt too uncomfortable to discuss the details of her past; but as she got to know her therapist better, she began to recall bits and pieces of her shattered childhood. The emotional pain during these discussions would sometimes cause Samantha to wring her hands or curl up into a ball. At other times, she would stop talking in the middle of a sentence and just stare off into space.

After nearly a year of therapy, personality alters began to emerge. Samantha was eventually diagnosed with a rare form of dissociative disorder called *multiple personality disorder*. One of the alter personalities identified herself as "Sky." Sky was shy and quiet and acted the age of about seven. Then there was "Sarah." She was sad and tearful, seemingly locked in a state of depression. A third alter identified herself as "Sam," "the protector." She was very critical and was reluctant to trust the therapist, sometimes even warning the other alters not to talk to the therapist. The most dramatic of the alters was "Sunny," who, in contrast to the others, was happy-go-lucky. She would typically emerge with a burst of laughter and a devilish look on her face. Then she would crack jokes, talk incessantly, and prance around the room.

As is typical of multiple personality disorder, Samantha, the persona, had no recall of what was said or done by her alters. The alter ego states represent parts of the psyche that have been split off from the core personality in a desperate effort to protect against painful emotions. They appear when the persona is under emotional stress and dissociates (runs away mentally) as a defense against uncomfortable thoughts and feelings. That is why Samantha had no recollection of what had occurred during a dissociative episode. Naturally, this created significant difficulty in her social and occupational functioning. The goal of therapy would be to earn the trust of each of Samantha's ego states, while at the same time giving her the skills and maturity to eliminate her need to dissociate.

Samantha's treatment was further complicated by the emotional abuse that she continued to receive from her fiancé. The stress caused intermittent threats of suicide by "Sarah" and acts of violence by "Sam." On one occasion, Sarah took an overdose, and Samantha was hospitalized.

Having never seen a case of multiple personality disorder, the attending psychiatrist was initially skeptical about the diagnosis. But during an office visit with Samantha, he met one of her alters, an experience that caused him to think more seriously about the therapist's diagnosis. After several more visits with the patient and a comprehensive review of the case, the doctor added a diagnosis of major depressive disorder, and started Samantha on Effexor.

Approximately one week later, Samantha's husband accompanied her to a therapy session and told the therapist that Samantha had developed difficulty sleeping; she had also spent over three thousand dollars on unneeded clothing. Although Samantha admitted to difficulty sleeping, she had no memory of purchasing the clothes.

The following week, Samantha met with the therapist alone. During the meeting, the therapist again inquired about the shopping spree. This time, Samantha began to space out...and suddenly Sunny burst out in devilish laughter. She was louder and more aggressive than usual as she boisterously described all the clothes she had bought. Then she abruptly disappeared, and Samantha returned with a confused look on her face. Even with prompting by the therapist, Samantha had no recall of what Sunny had said and continued to deny having bought the clothes.

Concerned that the antidepressant might be pushing Samantha into mania, the therapist contacted the psychiatrist and discussed her concerns that Samantha might be bipolar. Upon further review, the psychiatrist discontinued Effexor and started Samantha on Depakote. After approximately one week, Samantha started sleeping better. Also, the therapist noticed that Samantha was dissociating less.

During a therapy session approximately three months later, "Sam," the protector, appeared. She expressed anger and distrust toward the psychiatrist because the new medication was causing her to gain weight. The therapist gently encouraged Sam to discuss the problem with her psychiatrist. The therapist also spoke with the psychiatrist prior to Samantha's meeting with him.

At Samantha's office visit, the doctor asked her if she was having any side effects from the Depakote. Although Samantha mentioned the weight gain, she was not assertive enough to complain. Then suddenly Sam appeared and demanded that the medication be discontinued. The doctor fielded Sam's complaint calmly and explained that the acid derivative of Depakote, called Depakene (valproic acid) could be substituted in an effort to avoid weight gain.

The medication change was successful and helped increase Samantha's trust and respect for the doctor.

Over the next several years, the therapist and the doctor continued to collaborate in their efforts to help Samantha. As her coping skills improved, Samantha began to dissociate less. Her growing trust of the therapist also made way for the reintegration of the split parts of her personality.

The success of Samantha's treatment provided valuable insights into the relationship between her abusive past, the electrochemical abnormality in her brain, and the rare disorder that she had developed. From what is known about the relationship between stress and bipolar disorder, the emotional stress of Samantha's abusive childhood would have magnified her bipolarity. At the same time, her bipolarity would have magnified the emotional trauma of her abusive past. This vicious cycle would have driven Samantha's need to dissociate—and with increasing frequency and duration over time. Eventually, Samantha's dissociative episodes were of sufficient frequency and duration to permit the development of not only one but several split personalities, each representing a distinct attitude and behavior pattern that Samantha felt was unsafe to realize consciously. Hence, her alter personalities were allowed to express themselves but only without Samantha's conscious awareness; that is, while she was dissociating.

Moreover, each of her alters could be linked to one or another of the various mood states that characterize bipolar disorder. "Sky," the shy, quiet alter, could be linked to times when Samantha was in a frightened emotional state; "Sarah," the sad, tearful alter, could be linked to times when Samantha was in a depressed state; "Sam," the protector, could be linked to times when Samantha was irritable and anxious; and "Sunny," the boisterous, pleasure seeker, could be linked to times when Samantha was manic or hypomanic.

Samantha's progress in psychotherapy was facilitated when her bipolar disorder was adequately treated with medication, thereby bringing into a normal range her emotional responses to thoughts and experiences. This both facilitated and augmented the development of healthier and more mature psychological defense mechanisms, which in turn reduced the need for Samantha to dissociate. Meanwhile, the trust that each of her alters developed in the therapist allowed them to feel safe enough to reintegrate, thus allowing Samantha to move toward a state of emotional wholeness.

In the past, lack of understanding about the brain's influence on the mind left analysts and psychotherapists attempting to treat patients who had a dual diagnosis (psychological plus neurochemical abnormality) as if the entire problem were intrapsychic. This markedly hindered progress in therapy, particularly in complex cases like this one. However, recent advances in neurobiology and psychopharmacology have made it possible for clinicians to treat abnormalities of the brain, thereby permitting treatment of the whole person, body and soul, in their efforts to correct emotional disorders.

EXPRESSION TEN
Bipolarity in Aging and Dementia

As discussed earlier, most persons with bipolar spectrum disorder are probably never properly diagnosed. In most cases, the emotional instability that characterizes the disorder is so subtle and similar to normal responses to psychosocial cues that neither the patient nor the clinician can distinguish between the two. The disorder is further camouflaged by the fact that the symptoms tend to be mild when the level of emotional and physical stress is low.

From time to time, however, stress on the emotional system can mount to levels that produce enough symptom instability to make the disorder apparent. A divorce, a loss of employment, a death in the family, can be like wind blowing over the water in their ability to kick up the waves of a cyclic mood disorder. Physical stress, such as an injury, a surgical procedure, a heart attack, an infection, or even an allergen can have a similar effect. Unfortunately, most persons with a cyclic mood disorder do not receive a formal psychiatric evaluation until one or a combination of the aforementioned stressors cause the condition to become more obvious. Even then, the condition is usually misdiagnosed as unipolar depression or is simply assumed to be due to the immediate crisis. Most patients do not have the insight to tell the doctor that their symptoms are cyclic, and most clinicians are still not accustomed to ruling out soft forms of bipolar disorder, particularly in the context of an acute physical illness or advancing age.

Consequently, the majority of bipolar patients who become acutely symptomatic due to emotional or physical stress continue to be misdiagnosed with major depression or dysthymia and treated with antidepressants. When antidepressants repeatedly fail, the patient is labeled "treatment resistant," and ECT is usually recommended. This scenario is particularly common in the elderly, who often lack the physical reserve to keep trying different antidepressants. ECT, like antidepressants, is either ineffective or only temporarily effective for most cyclic mood disorders. Unfortunately, there are many patients, both young and old, who have been misdiagnosed with classic depression and continually treated with ECT due to the clinician's failure to make the correct diagnosis and use mood stabilizers.

If an elderly person has senile dementia, the signs and symptoms of mood cycling, such as depression, poor concentration, and irritability can easily be misattributed to the dementia. The correct diagnosis is often not made until the emotional, psychological, and physical stresses of the dying process combine to trigger enough symptom instability to make the diagnosis clinically apparent. Misdiagnosed bipolar patients who also have senile dementia are commonly managed with major tranquilizers, such as Haldol (haloperidol) and Zyprexa (olonzapine), or minor tranquilizers, such as Ativan or Valium (diazepam). The option of trying a mood stabilizer is often never even considered. An interesting side note is that a decade ago, Depakote became a popular option for reducing agitation in the elderly, but its mechanism of action was unknown. Today, with increasing awareness of cyclic mood disorders, Depakote's mechanism of action would more likely be seen as mood stabilization via its anticonvulsant effect.

CLINICAL CASE VIGNETTE

Eighty-three-year-old man with senile dementia and nursing home placement following heart surgery and total hip replacement

An eighty-three-year-old retired foundry worker developed severe depressive symptoms approximately three months after cardiac bypass surgery. Prior to surgery, he had been relatively healthy with the exception of some mild memory loss. There was no prior history of depression, but his children described him as a "type A personality," who was very demanding of himself and others.

Because Harold's depressive symptoms included difficulty sleeping and a worsening of his back pain, his internist started him on a small dose of the antidepressant Amitriptyline. After two weeks on the medication, he was no better. Therefore, the medication was gradually increased. As the dosage approached 100mg per day, Harold developed lightheadedness, which he initially assumed to be heart-related.

At the end of the second month on the medication, Harold became dizzy and fell while getting up at night to go to the bathroom. His wife called an ambulance because he was in severe pain and unable to get off the floor. X-Rays in the emergency room showed a fracture of his right hip. Harold was admitted to the hospital and scheduled for hip surgery.

Although the operation went well, Harold developed confusion after surgery. At times he thought he was working in the foundry; at other times, he thought he was at home. A psychiatric consultation was ordered, and Harold was diagnosed with delirium, dementia, and major depressive disorder. Due to his poor response to Amitriptyline and concerns about medication side effects, Amitriptyline was discontinued and Cymbalta (duloxetine) was started. A low dose of Zyprexa was added to treat confusion and agitation. Harold was also started on Aricept (donepezil) for dementia.

Despite these medication changes, Harold remained confused and continued to experience symptoms of depression. The dosage of Zyprexa was increased, but without much improvement. Zyprexa was eventually discontinued and replaced with Haldol. As the Haldol dose was increased, Harold's agitation and confusion began to subside, but he became over-sedated. He also continued to be very depressed, and so He was transferred to the psychiatric unit.

Under the presumption that Harold was suffering from an agitated depression, Cymbalta was continued. After a total of one week on the medication, the dosage was increased but did not yield any improvement in Harold's depressive symptomatology. Cymbalta was eventually discontinued and replaced with the antidepressant Wellbutrin (bupropion). After one week, the dosage was increased, but again, there was no improvement. After a total of two weeks on Wellbutrin, the medication was discontinued and replaced with the antidepressant Effexor. After one week, the dosage was increased, but Harold started to become more agitated.

In light of Harold's poor response to antidepressants and the negative effect that his depressive symptoms were having on his recovery from surgery, the option of ECT was discussed with Harold and his wife. The couple was shown a video about the procedure and an effort was made to answer all their questions. Harold eventually consented to the procedure, and over the next three weeks he underwent a total of nine ECT treatments.

Harold tolerated the first few treatments well, but after the fourth treatment, he began to experience increasing confusion and memory loss. The doctor reassured Harold that the memory loss was likely temporary and that it was important to complete the full course of ECT. Unfortunately, however, even after completing all nine ECT treatments, Harold had little improvement in his depressive symptomatology.

Due to the tenacity of Harold's depression, the doctor consulted with another psychiatrist. As part of the evaluation, the consulting psychiatrist obtained a thorough family history, including interviews with Harold's wife and children. In order to rule out the possibility that Harold was suffering from a cyclic mood disorder, all family members were carefully questioned about any evidence of mood instability in Harold's past. Harold's wife was unable to recall any such symptoms, but his daughter pointed out one type of inconsistency: Harold's temperament was unpredictable. At times, he could be polite and easygoing; at other times, he could be critical and demanding. Harold's son chided in, saying that most of the time he was the latter. Upon further questioning, family members began to sight other inconsistencies in Harold's mood, energy, and behavior. This led to a presumptive diagnosis of cyclic depression. The doctor reasoned that Harold's depressive symptoms may have been exacerbated by his heart surgery and further complicated by the stress of his hip fracture and second surgery. The doctor explained that Harold's mood had probably been unstable since his teens, but that the symptoms had never become severe enough to cause obvious trouble until he underwent the stress of his heart surgery. This, he said, would also explain why the antidepressants had more of an agitating effect than an antidepressant effect.

With that, Effexor was discontinued and Depakote was started. Harold tolerated the medication well, but no improvement was noticed until the doctor began to reduce the Haldol dosage. As Haldol was reduced, Harold became less sedated but remained calm. He also seemed to be more animated and less depressed. As the dosage of Depakote was increased, Harold experienced further improvement.

Harold's family had never known him to be so pleasant. Harold was not only less depressed, but much of the agitation that was previously thought to be due to his dementia, had vanished. At a subsequent office visit, Harold's daughter asked where the medication had been all the years that her father had been so difficult.

+ + +

CHAPTER 4

―⧉―

CLASSIC (UNIPOLAR) DEPRESSION

Although the recognition and diagnosis of cyclic forms of depression, such as bipolar disorder, bipolar II disorder, cyclothymia, and cyclic depression is on the rise, unipolar forms of depression, which include major depressive disorder, dysthymia, and recurrent depression, still account for a small but significant percentage of depressed patients. In a retrospective chart review of three hundred patients who sought treatment for depression, I found that one out of five patients had the unipolar form. In light of the prevalence of unipolar depression and the fact that the treatment of this condition is different than that of bipolar disorder, it is important to distinguish unipolar depression from bipolar depression.

In contrast to bipolar depression, unipolar depression is characterized by symptoms that persist for months to years with relatively little fluctuation in type or severity. Classically, symptoms of depression, such as sadness, anxiety, and worries about the future develop so gradually that the affected person might think they are entirely due to emotional stress. Other symptoms, such as low motivation, poor concentration, and changes in sleep or weight are then assumed to be secondary to continued worry rather than signs of a mood disorder in evolution. Although words of encouragement from family and friends and efforts at self-care, such as rest, exercise, and stress reduction can be helpful, the sinequanon of a mood disorder is the stubborn persistence of symptoms despite all efforts to make things better.

Like cyclic mood disorders, unipolar mood disorders are caused by a neurochemical abnormality; hence, they require medical treatment. Antidepressants are the drugs of choice. Mood stabilizers are not very effective in the treatment of unipolar depression presumably because the system is already stable, albeit depressed. From the standpoint of the MCNH hypothesis, neuronal hyperexcitability in unipolar depression is too stable and persistent to respond to lithium or an anticonvulsant. Therefore, an antidepressant should be taken in an effort to selectively stimulate pleasure-producing circuits in the brain. The classic two to four week delay in response is presumably the time required for the medication's effects to override homeostatic mechanisms in the brain.

In a small percentage of cases, one antidepressant after another will fail to be effective, and the patient will be labeled "treatment resistant." In the majority of these cases, a cyclic depression has either been misdiagnosed as unipolar depression or coexists with a unipolar depression. In either case, the patient is apt to make little progress until the cyclic mood disorder is adequately treated with mood stabilizers. What is more, treating a cyclic depression with antidepressants can increase the severity of symptoms, increase cycling of symptoms, and, over time, lead to full-blown manic-depressive disorder. Recently, the FDA asked thirteen antidepressant manufacturers to include strong safety warnings about the use of antidepressants in the treatment of depression. The FDA has asked physicians to caution patients about the risks associated with antidepressant use and to closely monitor patients for the development or worsening of anxiety, irritability, insomnia, racing thoughts, and other symptoms, including suicidal ideation.

Clinical Case Vignette

Nineteen-year-old college student with a major depressive episode

This bright, athletic, healthy young man graduated from high school with academic honors and letters in three sports. He had accepted a football scholarship to a prestigious university and was in the middle of his first semester when he began to feel increasingly overwhelmed by the pressures of school.

Only weeks after the start of classes, he could see that the tremendous time commitment to football left virtually no time for his studies. Each day consisted of going directly from class to the football field. Then, by the time he returned to his dormitory and had dinner, he was usually too tired to do anything but go to sleep.

He soon learned that if he were to have any chance to survive academically, he would have to get all his studying done during the day. Although this effort was helpful, he continued to have difficulty keeping up. As time went on, he found himself falling further and further behind academically. Eventually, the emotional stress caused him to have difficulty sleeping at night, even though he felt physically exhausted. As he approached the end of his first semester, his lack of sleep began to affect his concentration, and he knew he was in trouble.

Fearing that he would either have to quit the football team or fail his classes, he began to break down emotionally. When he discussed the problem with his parents, his father sounded disappointed; having played college football himself, he was looking forward to seeing Troy do something he was unable to do because of a nagging knee injury. Troy's mother, on the other hand, thought he should quit playing football, take the rest of the semester off, and come home.

Troy's wishes to please his parents created even more distress, and the emotional tension progressed to the point where going to football practice felt like a burden, and sitting in class became unbearable.

At the recommendation of a teammate, Troy went to the student health department, where he was diagnosed with depression and referred to a local psychiatrist.

After taking a complete history, including an inquiry about any prior history of mood swings, racing thoughts, or energy fluctuations, the psychiatrist diagnosed Troy with major depressive disorder. He reassured Troy that the illness was temporary but that it could worsen if he did not begin treatment. With that, the doctor recommended that Troy begin psychotherapy in addition to an antidepressant and another medication for sleep. The doctor explained that the antidepressant would probably take ten to fourteen days to begin working but that the sleeping pill should start working immediately. He explained that restoration of sleep was half the battle in getting Troy well and that he should let him know if he were continuing to have insomnia.

Although Troy was desperate to get better, he dreaded the idea of taking medication. Psychotherapy perhaps…but psychotropic medication? And he felt unable to talk to his parents about it because they were from the "old school" and surely would not understand the idea of taking medication for emotional stress.

Feeling like he had nowhere else to turn, Troy again spoke to the friend who recommended that he go to the student health department. When he told him that the doctor had recommended an antidepressant and a sleeping pill, Jim said that his sister had a similar problem and did not get better until she started taking medication.

Jim's words gave Troy just enough encouragement to start taking the medication. After just a few days, Troy began to feel better. The medication helped him start sleeping through the night, and he began to feel less overwhelmed. Thanks to the medication and support he received, he managed to complete the semester and even continue playing football. At a subsequent office visit, the doctor recommended that Troy attempt to discontinue the sleeping pill but continue to take the antidepressant for the remainder of the academic year.

CLINICAL CASE VIGNETTE

Forty-eight-year-old man with major depressive disorder superimposed upon a cyclic mood disorder

A forty-eight-year-old man in his third marriage was brought to the emergency room after a self-inflicted gunshot wound to his head. On examination, he had brisk bleeding from the scalp but was conscious and somewhat coherent. Physical examination and x-rays of the head revealed no evidence of skull fracture, and a CAT scan showed no evidence of intracranial bleeding. Stat labs showed a high blood alcohol level, but the remainder of the drug screen was negative.

The man's wife said her husband Richard seemed upset earlier that evening but did not want to talk about it. Sometime after midnight, she was awoken by the sound of a gunshot. She called 911 after seeing her husband lying on the basement floor in a pool of blood.

After his scalp laceration was sutured in the emergency room, Richard was admitted to the hospital for observation and alcohol detoxification. A psychiatry consult was ordered, and he and his wife were interviewed separately the following day.

Richard told the psychiatrist that he felt as though his life were falling apart. He had been having problems at work, and when a large business investment he had secretly made fell through, he feared that he would not be able to make ends meet. That same night, after his wife went to bed, he tried to drown his feelings in alcohol, but he continued to feel hopeless. The only solution, he began to think, was to end his life so that his wife could collect his life insurance. So, out of desperation, he went down to the basement and loaded a handgun that he kept for protection.

Further history indicated that Richard was a hard-working commodities trader who enjoyed the excitement of the stock market and thrived on the challenge of having to make quick, high-risk decisions. He described himself as one who easily became bored and was easily distracted. However, the thrill of commodities trading held his attention. Thus, he preferred to spend most of his time at work, after which he would come home and have a few drinks to help him wind down. In recent years, he had been spending less and less time with his family and shamefully admitted that he had gotten himself into serious financial trouble.

During her interview with the psychiatrist, Richard's wife described her husband as a "high-strung workaholic" who did not know when to quit. Escalating tensions over his work schedule, his drinking, and his little time at home were driving her further and further away from him. Though she had not seen any depressive symptoms, she talked about Richard's anger in association with his drinking. When the doctor asked her to elaborate on this, she said that her husband would often fly into a rage over seemingly trivial things when under the influence of alcohol.

When the association between Richard's drinking and his anger was reviewed more closely, his wife was able to recall at least a few occasions on which Richard had blown things out of proportion despite not being under the influence of alcohol; during those times, he would typically pour himself a drink to calm down. Richard's wife was also able to recall a few times when Richard had been relatively easy-going and pleasant, even if he had been drinking.

Based upon the foregoing information, the psychiatrist concluded that Richard had a cyclic mood disorder that he had been self-medicating with alcohol. In this case, bipolar symptoms were manifesting themselves as anxiety and irritability. At times, alcohol was effective in relieving the symptoms; at other times, its sedative effects were outweighed by its disinhibiting effect, resulting in some of Richard's explosive episodes while under the influence.

After explaining this to the patient and his wife, the psychiatrist recommended a trial of mood stabilizers. The medication was intended to prevent the anxiety and irritability that were causing much of the trouble for Richard both at home and at work. His choice of work, his distractibility, and the impulsivity of his suicide attempt raised the possibility that he also had ADD.

The psychiatrist explained that treatment would need to proceed in stages. The first step would be to stabilize Richard's mood. After that, symptoms of ADD would be treated with psychostimulants. The order of treatment was important because psychostimulants can offset the calming effect of mood stabilizers, and mood instability can interfere with the therapeutic effect of psychostimulants. The doctor also recommended individual psychotherapy for Richard as well as marital therapy.

After several months of medication and psychotherapy, Richard's mood was stabilized and, with the help of psychostimulants, he was able to be more attentive to his wife. In addition, the reduction in his nervousness and irritability resulted in less tension at home and helped Richard remain abstinent from alcohol.

Just as things were beginning to improve, Richard began to experience bouts of chest pain and shortness of breath. Initially, he attributed the symptoms to acid reflux, a condition he had had for many years. But as symptoms progressed, his wife began to insist that he be reevaluated.

Due in part to worries about his medical expenses, Richard put off going to the doctor. Approximately three months later, while working in the yard, he collapsed, and his wife called for an ambulance.

In the emergency room, Richard was diagnosed with a mild heart attack. Further tests revealed severe obstruction of four of his coronary arteries, and surgery was recommended. Four days later, he underwent four-vessel coronary artery bypass graft surgery.

Although the operation went well, Richard had trouble coming off the ventilator and was becoming increasingly agitated. The possibility of alcohol withdrawal was considered, but Richard's wife felt confident that he had not been drinking in months. Because the patient was not responding to standard sedatives, a psychiatry consult was ordered.

The on-call psychiatrist took a complete history from the patient's wife, noting that Richard's mood stabilizer, Neurontin, had been discontinued when he was admitted to the hospital. The psychiatrist explained that the discontinuation of the medication, combined with the increased physical and emotional stress of Richard's surgery, was the most likely cause of the agitation he was experiencing in the intensive care unit.

The doctor restarted the Neurontin, and within an hour of the first dose, Richard became calm and cooperative. He was extubated the following day and, a few days later, he was discharged from the hospital.

However, approximately six weeks into his recovery, he began to backslide. He started to lose his appetite and become increasingly worried about his financial problems. This added to the worries that he already had about his heart. As the weeks went by, his tendency to oversleep changed to inability to sleep. He then became increasingly anxious and started to fear that he was going to have another heart attack. Shortly thereafter, he awoke in the middle of the night with shortness of breath and tightness in his chest. Fearing that he might be having another heart attack, his wife called an ambulance.

In the emergency room, test results, including an electro-cardiogram and cardiac enzymes, showed no evidence of arrhythmia or acute myocardial infarction. The emergency room doctor concluded that Richard was having a panic attack. Thus, he was given 2mg of Ativan and discharged with a recommendation to follow-up with his psychiatrist.

At the next office visit, the psychiatrist diagnosed Richard with major depression and panic disorder. The doctor explained that these conditions were superimposed upon the cyclic mood disorder for which he was already being treated and were probably triggered by the emotional and psychological strain of his heart attack and subsequent surgery. To treat the depressive disorder, the doctor recommended that an antidepressant be added temporarily. Zoloft was chosen because of its relatively low tendency to destabilize mood and its effectiveness in panic disorder. Richard's insomnia was treated with the benzodiazepine Restoril (temazepam).

With an effective mood stabilizer already in place, Richard responded well to the antidepressant. Within about ten days, his mood became brighter and his anxiety began to diminish. He continued to need Restoril for sleep, but he was able to discontinue it five weeks later. Henceforth he did not have another panic attack and eventually came to feel better than he had felt in years. The doctor explained that approximately half of all patients with cyclic mood disorders do better long-term if they remain on a combination of mood stabilizer and low-dose antidepressant. Low doses are generally better than high doses because of the tendency for antidepressants to destabilize mood in patients with cyclic mood disorders. With this in mind, Richard decided to remain on a low dose of Zoloft even after his depressive symptoms had completely resolved.

Comment

In this case, the added benefit of an antidepressant in a patient with a cyclic mood disorder was discovered serendipitously when the patient needed to be treated for a superimposed major depressive episode. The combination of mood stabilizer and low-dose antidepressant brought the patient to a higher level of functioning than he had been at in years. For Richard, the low-dose antidepressant would also tend to prevent future panic attacks, a benefit that is especially important because of the potential for cardiac chest pain to be confused with panic attacks and vice-versa.

+ + +

CHAPTER 5

—⟨⟨⟩⟨⟩⟩—

THE ART AND SCIENCE OF TREATMENT

E ffective treatment begins with an accurate diagnosis. Teachers of medicine say that ninety percent of the diagnosis is found in the patient's history. Nowhere is this more true than in the field of psychiatry, where there are very few tests available to help the doctor determine the cause of the patient's symptoms. Therefore, it is paramount that the patient and the physician work together to carefully reconstruct the history of the presenting illness. Whenever possible, family members, friends, and others who know the patient well should supplement the history that the patient provides, including a detailed family history. In an era of managed care and intensive efforts to reduce health care costs, clinicians are inclined to hurry from one patient to another at the risk of failing to obtain a complete and accurate history.

In psychiatry, the first diagnostic challenge is to determine whether there is a biological component to the patient's symptoms. This is a crucial step in the evaluation because biologically based symptoms are best treated biologically, whereas psychologically based symptoms are best treated psychologically. That is not to say that there is no place for psychotherapy in the treatment of neurochemical disorders. In fact, because neurochemical abnormalities of the brain are often precipitated by psychological stress, psychotherapy can be very helpful. However, once the brain's neurochemical functioning becomes dysregulated, psychotherapy is not nearly as fast and effective as medical treatment in restoring normal brain function.

The treatment of psychological causes of psychiatric symptoms, as in grief, neuroses, and personality disorders, involves helping the patient accept loss or achieve a change in attitude. Although numerous methods of doing this have been proposed by theorists such as Sigmund Freud, Carl Young, James Masterson, and Aaron Beck, the most important first step is to call upon the great physician Jesus Christ. Those who call upon Him receive the Holy Spirit, who has the intelligence and the power to help us overcome any difficulty, whether physical, emotional, or situational. This is not a religious solution but a spiritual one, and what could be more appropriate for the spiritual problem that intrapsychic distress is? The moment we place our faith in Jesus Christ, the Holy Spirit begins to give us the ideas, the people, and the power to overcome any obstacle. That does not discount the value of psychological theories and medical treatments. On the contrary, it coordinates, facilitates, and perfects them as God leads us to those who can help us, be they psychologists, psychiatrists, or others, and He helps them to help us. All the while, He gives us the faith, the hope, and the love to stay the course.

If the patient's symptoms are believed to be partially or largely due to a neurochemical abnormality, then the nature of the abnormality should be determined and the proper medical treatment, applied. Since our emphasis is on mood disorders, we will limit our discussion to the two primary mood disorders, unipolar and bipolar depression.

If a unipolar depression is suspected, symptoms of bipolarity should be ruled out and a trial of antidepressants should be recommended. Typically, a treatment response takes seven to twenty-one days. Some doctors will raise the dosage of the antidepressant if there are no side effects and there is no evidence of improvement after ten to fourteen days. If significant side effects develop before there is any improvement, the medication should be discontinued and replaced with a different antidepressant. Some patients require trials of several different antidepressants before they experience improvement. The reason is that antidepressants exert their therapeutic effect by binding to receptors in the brain, and the exact size, structure, and spacial configuration of each person's receptors are as unique as the individual. Hence, finding the right antidepressant is like looking for the right sized pair of shoes. In addition, not all antidepressants work by the same mechanism or mechanisms. Consequently, some individuals may respond better to one antidepressant than another; others may benefit from combining different antidepressants. Importantly, an early treatment response, an exaggerated treatment response, an inconsistent treatment response, a worsening of symptoms, or a need to increase the dosage of antidepressant medication over time is suggestive of bipolarity and warrants a more careful review of the patient's individual and family history for evidence of bipolar disorder. Any personal or family history of mania or cycling of symptoms is warning enough to discontinue antidepressant therapy and begin a mood stabilizer. Because antidepressants can exacerbate the symptoms of a cyclic mood disorder and possibly worsen its course, it is safer to make the mistake of assuming that the patient has a bipolar disorder and treat with a mood stabilizer than to make the mistake of assuming that the patient has a treatment-resistant depression and continue to treat with antidepressants. Therefore, even the slightest suspicion of bipolarity warrants a trial of mood stabilizers.

If a bipolar disorder is suspected, a mood stabilizer should be prescribed. Unlike treating unipolar depression with an antidepressant, treating a cyclic mood disorder with a mood stabilizer yields immediate results (once the dosage is correct). This is because mood stabilizers work by a different mechanism in the treatment of bipolar disorders than do antidepressants in the treatment of unipolar disorders. However, most patients do not become aware of the therapeutic effect of a mood stabilizer until several cycles of anxiety, depression, or irritable mania have been prevented. Thus, the perceived therapeutic effect depends upon the length and frequency of the patient's cycles. Rapid cyclers generally become aware of improvement more quickly than non-rapid cyclers. If significant side effects develop before there is any improvement, the medication should be discontinued and replaced with an alternative mood stabilizer. As with antidepressants, mood stabilizers exert their therapeutic effects by binding to receptors in the brain, and each person's receptors are as unique as the individual. Therefore, as with antidepressants, some individuals might respond better to one mood stabilizer than to another. Others might benefit from combining different mood stabilizers.

In addition, the dosage of an antidepressant or mood stabilizer must be adjusted in order to balance the system. Each time a new medication is introduced, the neurochemical balance shifts in one direction or another. Therefore, finding the right dosage of a medication is often as important as the type of medication. In many cases, the proper medication is mistakenly discontinued either because the dosage was too low to be effective or so high that it produced unwanted side effects or even paradoxical (reverse) effects. In addition to these barriers to effective treatment, the brain has a natural tendency to resist change or partially compensate for the effects of medication. Consequently, more than one medication is often needed in order to maintain a therapeutic response. Although using a single medication is always more desirable than polypharmacy, combining medications at low dosage tends to produce fewer side effects and is usually more effective than overshooting the therapeutic dosage of a single medication. The efficacy of most medications is greatest at low doses, with a tendency toward diminishing returns and increasing side effects as the dosage is increased and receptors in the brain become saturated. There is still a misperception that psychotropic drugs will cause a person to feel over-sedated or turn one into "a zombie." But unlike in the past, modern day psychotropic medications are specifically designed to produce therapeutic effects and relatively few side effects. Hence, there is seldom a case in which the newer medications, when prescribed at the minimum therapeutic dosage, cause distressing side effects.

The success rate of any given antidepressant in the treatment of *properly diagnosed* unipolar depression is very high—approximately seventy percent. This is in contrast to some studies that have found a lower success rate or even no benefit over placebo. However, such studies have likely included a significant number of misdiagnosed bipolar spectrum patients. In any case, given that there are some twenty-five antidepressants currently available, the chance of successfully treating a true unipolar depression is close to one hundred percent. For cyclic mood disorders, the success rate for any given mood stabilizer is lower—approximately thirty percent. But with the availability of some fifteen mood stabilizers, the chance of treatment success is still well above ninety percent.

The process of trying different medications typically involves choosing one whose side effect profile is tolerable or, better yet, beneficial and then gradually increasing the dosage until there is either evidence of improvement or the side effects outweigh the therapeutic effects. For example, if one of the patient's symptoms is insomnia, we might begin by prescribing a sedating mood stabilizer at night, and then gradually increase the dosage to improve sleep and normalize mood. On the other hand, if tiredness were part of the presenting problem, we would try to avoid using medications that cause sedation.

Unless the symptoms are unusually extreme or unresponsive, only one medication adjustment should be made at a time. This systematic approach makes evident which medication or dosage adjustment was responsible for any improvement or side effects that occur. In many cases, one medication will yield partial improvement. If there is a need for further improvement, a second medication can be added. Unless there are side effects, substituting medications should be avoided because of the potential confusion created by making two changes at once. If the addition of a second medication yields further improvement, the first medication could be tapered and possibly discontinued if the second medication remains effective. In some cases, no single medication provides complete symptom relief. In such cases, combining medications might be necessary in order to alleviate the symptoms of a mood disorder.

In the treatment of bipolar depression, approximately fifty percent of patients benefit from the addition of an antidepressant to the mood stabilizer. The reason is that some patients become emotionally stable but remain depressed with mood stabilizer monotherapy. If an antidepressant is added to the mood stabilizer, it should be done cautiously and at low dose to avoid offsetting the mood stabilizing effect of the mood stabilizer. Of even more importance is to avoid treating bipolar disorder with an antidepressant alone because of the risk of further destabilizing mood and producing mania or more severe depression.

This leads to a commonly asked question: do antidepressants and mood stabilizers need to be taken on a long-term basis? For some forms of depression, such as unipolar depression and seasonal affective disorder, an antidepressant can be taken for a limited time (two to six months) and then discontinued. If symptoms return, the medication can be restarted. In contrast, bipolar disorders tend to be chronic. Symptoms generally begin during late childhood or early adolescence, peak during early adulthood, and wax and wane for the remainder of the person's life. This does not necessarily mean that there is no way to overcome the problem or that every patient must take medication for the rest of his or her life. Each person is different. Some patients may have lengthy periods of remission during which they can reduce or discontinue their medication; others may have such mild symptoms that medication becomes necessary only when the waves of the mood disorder are stirred up by severe psychological stress, a physical illness, or postpartum hormonal changes; still others may choose not to take medication at all, an option that belongs to every patient unless there is a legal stipulation that requires them to remain on medication. Some patients incorporate prayer, meditation, and other spiritual exercises that take stress off the brain and promote health and healing by channeling positive energy. I personally believe that the treatment of any illness can be aided by and potentially overcome through faith and prayer. However, spirituality is extremely personal, and only some patients are inclined to incorporate faith in the healing process. Most patients with a cyclic mood disorder benefit from and prefer long-term use of mood stabilizers because they tend to experience an immediate or eventual return of symptoms if they discontinue the medication. Furthermore, early diagnosis and continuous treatment can help prevent complications of depression, such as low self-esteem, self-neglect, and other behaviors that further jeopardize one's health, one's relationships, and one's life. Therefore, early intervention followed by continuous, long-term treatment of a cyclic mood disorder can be the difference between a healthy and productive life and an early loss of life.

Antiepileptic mood stabilizers are relatively safe to take and are non-addictive, but long-term use can lead to a deficiency of some important nutrients, including vitamin B12, vitamin B6, vitamin D, vitamin E, folic acid, calcium, selenium, zinc, and copper. Therefore, patients on long-term therapy should try to make good dietary choices and consider taking a daily multivitamin-mineral formula supplement. Those taking lithium are at risk of toxicity if they become severely dehydrated. That is not to say that they need to drink extra water, but the medication should be temporarily discontinued if there is excessive fluid loss from such things as persistent sweating, vomiting, or diarrhea.

The mood stabilizers that are currently available are lithium carbonate (Lithobid, Lithium Eskalith, Lithium Eskalith CR), valproic acid (Depakene, Divalproex sodium, Depakote, Depakote ER), carbamazepine (Tegretol, Tegretol XR, Carbitrol, Equetro), oxcarbazepine (Trileptal), gabapentin (Neurontin), pregabalin (Lyrica), topiramate (Topamax), tiagabine (Gabitril), lamotrigine (Lamictal), levetiracetam (Keppra), and zonisamide (Zonegran). All of these medications, with the exception of lithium, are listed as anticonvulsants in the Physician's Desk Reference (PDR) and related texts. Little reference is made to their mood stabilizing and anti-anxiety effects because all the anticonvulsants were originally developed and marketed for the treatment of epilepsy.

Other medications that have demonstrated mood-stabilizing effects include the six "atypical" antipsychotic medications, risperidone (Risperdal), olonzapine (Zyprexa), quetiapine fumarate (Seroquel, Seroquel XR), ziprazidone (Geodon), aripiprazole (Abilify), and clozapine (Clozaril). The older "typical" antipsychotics, such as chlorpromazine (Thorazine) and thioridazine (Mellaril) are useful also, but due to their side effects, they are usually used third-line. Both the atypical and the typical antipsychotic medications have more significant side effects than the traditional mood stabilizers (lithium and the anticonvulsants), especially when used long-term. Hence, they should be avoided unless the symptoms are unusually extreme or unresponsive to the traditional mood stabilizers.

In many cases, bipolar spectrum disorder is complicated by another disorder such as panic disorder, attention-deficit disorder, or obsessive-compulsive disorder. In such cases, treatment should proceed in stages, beginning with a mood stabilizer because the medications used to treat the aforementioned co-morbid disorders have a stimulating effect, which can further destabilize mood in the absence of an effective mood stabilizer. Furthermore, mood stabilizers are sometimes effective against co-morbid anxiety disorders and difficulties with concentration.

If a cyclic mood disorder is complicated by alcoholism or another substance of abuse, treatment of the mood disorder is facilitated by abstinence, both because substances of abuse tend to mask the symptoms of a cyclic mood disorder and because they tend to block the therapeutic effect of mood stabilizers. Yet because most persons who abuse alcohol and other drugs are self-medicating, the initiation of pharmacotherapy will sometimes need to precede abstinence. Unless hospitalized, most persons are either unable or unwilling to give up remedies to which they have become accustomed, even if those remedies are unhealthy for them. If a mood stabilizer is taken in combination with a substance of abuse, the therapeutic effect of the medication might still provide enough symptom relief to convince the patient that taking a scientifically formulated, doctor-prescribed medication is healthier than continuing to abuse their self-prescribed drug of choice. Notwithstanding, every patient should make an effort to maintain a brief period of abstinence when starting a mood stabilizer. This allows for a more accurate assessment of the drug's effect and maximizes the chances of a favorable response.

A commonly overlooked phenomenon in unipolar depressive disorders, bipolar disorders, and a variety of associated conditions, including fibromyalgia, irritable bowel syndrome, and migraine headaches, is the effect of the change of season. During the spring and the fall, many patients experience an exacerbation of their symptoms for several weeks or months. A subgroup of depression sufferers routinely experience symptoms that are confined to the fall and winter months. This phenomenon had originally been described as seasonal affective disorder (SAD), but recent studies indicate that the seasonal effect can also occur in the spring and is a more general phenomenon that affects up to ninety percent of the population at one time or another. Although the symptoms are most commonly neuropsychiatric, they can also be physical in nature, usually involving the most vulnerable parts of the body. Hence, the symptoms are typically a reemergence or exacerbation of symptoms one has had in the past. The association between the change of season and the activation of emotional and physical symptoms had long been unrecognized because of poor patient insight, clinician oversight, and "skip years," during which a person is relatively unaffected. The physiological mechanism behind the seasonal effect is unclear but appears to involve changes in the sun's brightness as the seasons change. It is probably also related to activity changes in the earth's geomagnetic field caused by the moon's orbit around the earth, the earth's orbit around the sun, and solar flares. The earth's geomagnetic field has three seasonal peaks: one from March to May, another in July, and the last in October. The pineal gland of the brain receives signals from the suprachiasmatic nucleus, which is sensitive to sunlight. But the pineal gland, which regulates circadian rhythm and melatonin production, is also sensitive to magnetic fields. Changes in input to the pineal gland, whether from changes in the sun's brightness, from magnetic field changes, or from an inconsistent sleep schedule can disrupt body clocks, thus putting susceptable individuals at risk for mood disorders. Electromagnetic fields, which have the power to trigger muscle twitches when placed over a person's skull and which rule the tides, could also have a direct effect on neurons, causing them to be hyperactive. Neuronal hyperactivity can have effects throughout the body and, as previously discussed, appear to underly a variety of psychiatric syndromes. The term "looney" comes from the long-held association between a full moon and temporary insanity in susceptible individuals.

Because the seasonal effect is temporary, treatment can be temporary for those whose symptoms are strictly seasonal. Those with bipolar spectrum disorder or dysthymia who experience a seasonal exacerbation of symptoms can increase the dosage of their medication or add another medication during the transitional period (usually between August and December, in the fall, and between March and May, in the spring). Once the transitional period is over, most patients can and should resume their previous treatment regimen.

A possible alternative or addition to medication for patients who experience the seasonal effect is light therapy. Based on the theory that changes in the sun's intensity at the change of season can affect circadian rhythm and brain chemicals that are linked to mood, daily exposure to bright light that mimics natural outdoor light has been studied and found to be helpful for some patients. There are a variety of Light Boxes and bulbs on the market, but in order to be effective, the brightness must be in the range of 10,000 lux. That's about one hundred times brighter than a 100-watt bulb. Moving towards or away from the light changes the intensity level. Light box brightness levels can vary between manufacturers, so check to find the particular 10,000 lux distance range of your Light Box.

A typical treatment involves remaining within the prescribed distance of the Light Box for about thirty minutes soon after awakening and occasionally glancing (not staring) at the light. A response usually begins within two to four treatments, but it can take several weeks to receive the maximum benefit. Some persons can skip treatments for one to three days without a loss of effect, but most persons experience a return of symptoms when treatment is interrupted. Once adjusted to light therapy, most persons get a feel for the results and soon learn to adjust the session length and frequency to achieve an optimal therapeutic effect.

Light therapy does not work for everyone. Up to fifty percent of those diagnosed with SAD do not gain adequate relief from it, and symptoms that occur in the spring may be related more to the change in sunlight than to the loss of sunlight or to changes in the earth's geomagnetic field. Also, commercial Light Boxes are not regulated by law, so medical consultation and caution is advised when selecting and using them.

+ + +

CHAPTER 6

※

MORAL AND RELIGIOUS ASPECTS
OF TREATMENT

For many people, the idea of taking medication that affects thoughts and feelings creates a moral dilemma: will the medicine take away my emotions? will it change my personality? will it change who I am? These and other such questions represent fears about losing one's identity, one's relationships, and one's soul through the use of psychotropic drugs.

For some, the use of psychotropic medication also raises important spiritual and religious questions. Those who have been raised in a faith-based home or a religious community might wonder whether it is right to take drugs like antidepressants, mood stabilizers, and tranquilizers to feel better; or are we, through the use of these chemicals, attempting to change our God-given nature and our natural response to life's ups and downs? Some religious communities believe that any form of medical intervention, even if it were emergent, would be interfering with God's plan for our lives.

Years before I entered the field of medicine, I served as a Chaplain's Aide at the UCLA Medical Center. As I was contemplating becoming a doctor, I asked the hospital Chaplain, Fr. Patrick Traynor, whether God would rather have us rely upon doctors or upon Him when we become sick. Fr. Traynor gave me a simple, direct answer. God, he said, has many ways of helping us; one of them is through others, and sometimes that includes doctors and nurses. His answer gave me the reassurance that pursuing a career in medicine was potentially a good thing.

After becoming a physician of the mind, I began to realize that I was not only treating the body; I was also treating the soul. This discovery set me on a path of spiritual study and personal reflection that both complemented and surpassed my study of science and medicine. After twelve years of treating some patients with psychotropic medication, some with standard psychotherapy, and some with spiritually based psychotherapy, depending upon the needs and wishes of the patient, I am prepared to expound upon Fr. Traynor's comment.

I believe that in the eyes of God, every problem and challenge that we face is an opportunity to share God's love. Emotional and physical suffering might be part of the human condition, but the love we share in attempting to relieve it is our highest calling. We live up to that calling when we show a willingness to help those in need. I believe this is true regardless of the terminology or methodology we use, provided that the recipient is willing to receive it and that it enriches his or her life. Thus, the answer to the question, Does God approve of doctors prescribing psychotropic medications? depends upon three factors. The first is the patient's willingness to take them; the second is the doctor's willingness to prescribe them; and the third is the ability of the treatment to enrich the patient's life.

In the case of mental and emotional disorders, the patient's willingness to take medication is not a given. Due to the stigma of mental illness and the varied perceptions and attitudes about psychotropic drugs, many patients are conflicted about taking medication even if they think it might help them feel better. The second prerequisite to God's approval of medical-psychiatric treatment, the doctor's willingness to provide the treatment, is not a given either. For a physician to simply offer treatment is not enough to earn the patient's trust and cooperation. A doctor must convince the patient that he truly cares; and to do that, he must truly be willing to help. Such an attitude helps forge the kind of trusting relationship between the doctor and the patient that attracts God's favor. Last, but equally important, is the potential for the treatment to enrich the patient's life. That is, to improve the patient's quality of life and ability to function as a contributing member of society. Mood disorders can interfere with one's ability to relate to others and establish healthy relationships. In many cases, the sufferer is either completely incapacitated or so busy battling his or her illness that the individual has no emotional energy left for others. For this reason, many persons with mood, anxiety, and other emotional disorders are perceived as being self-centered and are rejected by society. Conversely, emotional illness can cause the sufferer to reject society. God's will is that all of us work together to make the world a better place. Therefore, if both the physician and the patient are willing, and the treatment has the potential to make everyone's world a better place, it stands to reason that God would support it.

Unfortunately, many persons who suffer from emotional disorders perceive treatment as a crutch. Enslaved by stereotypes from an era in which there was little understanding of psychiatric disorders and few treatment options available, they view psychotropic medications as mind-altering substances that threaten to alter their personality and produce nasty side effects. Most people do not understand the difference between the brain and the soul, nor do they understand the complex mechanisms by which the new generation of antidepressants, anticonvulsants, and antipsychotics normalize brain function.

As discussed earlier, a human being is more than just a sack of chemical reactions and neurological reflexes. A person is a spiritual being clothed with the flesh. Each of us is a separate soul who uses the brain to interact with the physical world, just as we use a computer to interact with the computer world. Psychotropic medications treat the brain, not the soul; they repair the computer, not the computer operator. Hence, receiving medication and other forms of somatic treatment for a neuropsychiatric disorder is like having one's computer repaired.

Because each person's brain is different, each medication must be tailored to the individual in order to be effective. In the past, treating psychiatric disorders was clumsy at best, both because our understanding of brain chemistry was rudimentary and because there were relatively few medications available. Today, there are some twenty-five antidepressants, ten mood stabilizers, and thirteen antipsychotics. The newest of these medications are highly specific, which means that they can correct abnormalities in brain function without disrupting those parts of the brain and body that are functioning normally. Consequently, they have fewer side effects. Of course, any medication has the potential to cause undesirable effects, but when prescribed for the right person, at the right dosage, and in the right combination, the new line of psychotropic medications can provide enormous benefits for those who suffer from emotional disorders.

God's will is that we work together to improve the quality of our lives. As a loving God, He is not as concerned with our methods as with the process by which we employ them. When the treatment is administered with love in the field of psychiatry, it is God in action both because of the manner in which it is administered and because effective treatment tends to improve the patient's relationships with others. The ultimate purpose of life on earth is to practice love toward one another. It stands to reason that God would like any barriers to that process, including emotional disorders, to be removed.

+ + +

CHAPTER 7

—⁂—

MOOD DISORDERS:
PAST, PRESENT, & FUTURE

L ike most physical illnesses, mood disorders were probably as common during ancient times as they are today. But like so many illnesses, advances in diagnosis and treatment make them appear to be more common in modern times. In the last fifty years, the diagnosis of bipolar disorder has been on the rise due to advances in treatment and our ability to distinguish it from other forms of depression. In addition, many patients who previously would have been diagnosed with schizophrenia have become more accurately diagnosed as having a mood disorder (primarily bipolar) with psychotic features. Beyond that, the latest research suggests that schizophrenia might not be a distinct entity at all but rather another manifestation of bipolar disorder. Added to this is the growing awareness that classic bipolar disorder is just the tip of the iceberg in the spectrum of cyclic mood disorders. Clinicians and researchers from around the world are rapidly discovering that soft forms of the disorder, including bipolar II, cyclothymia, cyclic depression, depressive mixed states, and hyperthymic temperament, are very common in the general population. What is the relevance of this? Cyclic mood disorders may be as common as high blood pressure—and just as easy to treat if we can learn to recognize them in our family members, friends, and coworkers.

The problem of recognition is threefold. First is the stigma of mental illness; second is a failure to recognize symptoms; and third is the lack of education about the causes and available treatments. Unlike other medical illnesses, psychiatric illness carries a stigma. The stigma of mental illness dates back to the earliest recorded history, when the mentally ill were labeled, mocked, and rejected by society. Due to a lack of understanding about mental illness, priests and healers tried to scare the mentally ill into sanity and perform exorcisms in an effort to rid them of demons. During medieval times, they were burned at the stake to ensure that they did not contaminate others physically or spiritually. One can only imagine the contempt and humiliation that a manic person who was psychotic or religiously preoccupied would have received in the days of yore.

The negative sentiment about mental illness has been passed from generation to generation until today, when most persons are still reluctant to consider the idea that they, a family member, or a friend might be in need of psychiatric treatment. Those who are successfully treated are often hesitant to share their experience due to the continued stigma of mental illness.

Coupled with the shame of mental illness is the second barrier to diagnosis: failure to recognize symptoms. Because neurochemical abnormalities can create the same psychological, emotional, and behavioral symptoms that loss and disappointment create, the two are often confused with each other. In the absence of objective criteria by which to make the distinction, a sufferer would naturally prefer an explanation that permits him or her to externalize the blame and remain in control. A psychosocial explanation does just that—it allows one to say: I am not the problem; but even if I am, I can change without any help. Hence, it can be quite difficult to convince someone that the problem is more than just psychological.

Then there is the lack of education about the causes of mental illness and the available treatments. Most people continue to think that emotional problems are entirely embedded in one's personality. It is counterintuitive to think that natural feelings, such as anxiety, depression, anger, and other emotions with which all of us are familiar can also be caused by a neurochemical abnormality—a physical abnormality in the brain over which I have limited control. Hence, most families who are plagued by mood disorders either fail or refuse to seek medical help. Instead, they are inclined to argue with one another and point the finger. This increases the risk of avoidance behavior such as drinking, gambling, sexual indiscretion, eating disorders, and other self-destructive behaviors that are personal choices and, hence, further obscure the fact that there is an underlying problem over which they have limited control. To the bewilderment of parents and teachers, many bright, talented, highly motivated adolescents suddenly and for no apparent reason lose interest in their usual activities, become truant from school, and join the drug culture. Misattribution of these behaviors to pure freedom of choice prevents many families from recognizing the onset of a mood disorder that needs prompt medical attention. Even when obvious psychiatric symptoms emerge, they are often misattributed to drug abuse and the unhealthy lifestyle that their child has adopted. Consequently, many adolescents receive blame and criticism rather than appropriate treatment. Bars, drug houses, and prisons are filled with persons who are suffering from undiagnosed psychiatric conditions such as bipolar disorder, chronic depression, and ADD. Most of these individuals were likely raised by parents and grandparents who were afflicted with the same condition that they unknowingly passed to their children. The combination of genetic factors and dysfunctional family dynamics plagues many families for generations.

Further complicating the problem of diagnosis is the challenge of treatment. The human mind is the most complex aspect of a human being and the final frontier of medicine. Science has mastered every other part of the body—the heart, the lung, the liver, and the kidney. These and many other body parts have either been transplanted or artificially engineered from metals and plastics. Yet until now, the mind has remained an enigma to science. Consequently, mental health practitioners have made many blunders and devised some desperate treatments that have done more harm than good. The image of psychiatry continues to be tainted by these failed attempts. Added to this are the frightening stories that some have heard about a friend or a family member who was chronically over-medicated or became permanently scarred through psychiatric treatment.

Happily, all of this is rapidly changing. Over the past two decades, advances in psychiatry and the availability of new medications that target specific receptors in the brain have brought miraculous cures and provided new insights into the workings of the human mind. This book is an effort to share the good news and unveil secrets of the mind that have been a mystery until now. It is a book of hope that is intended to help overcome long-standing barriers to diagnoses and treatment and help patients understand themselves better.

It is time that we stop assuming that mental and emotional problems are part of one's personality and that one just has to pull himself up by his bootstraps and get back into the game. It is time that we challenge old attitudes and take advantage of effective new treatments. We are living in an era in which miracles of healing are being performed every day through advances in science and medicine. At last, those miracles are beginning to include healing of one of the oldest ailments known to mankind—depression.

+ + +

ABOUT THE AUTHOR

MICHAEL R. BINDER, M.D., is a board-certified adult and adolescent psychiatrist who has been in practice for nearly twenty years. He earned his bachelor's degree from UCLA and his medical degree from the University of Chicago, Pritzker School of Medicine. In 1992 he completed a four-year residency program in psychiatry at the Medical College of Wisconsin and received an award for outstanding research.

In addition to establishing a busy private practice, Dr. Binder became active in teaching and administration. He has trained medical students and residents, lectured on mood disorders, and served as Chairman of the Department of Psychiatry at Waukesha Memorial Hospital.

After several years in practice, the complexities of mental and emotional disorders led him to an extensive study of the human spirit. This led to a better understanding of the relationship between the brain and the soul and to the development of a psychopharmacological treatment approach that has nearly doubled his success in treating patients with mood disorders. He is the author of three books: *Am I Depressed Or Am I Bipolar, Images of Heaven: A Book of Love, Wisdom & Truth,* and *Miracles: Ask and Ye Shall Receive.*

In 2005, he founded The Binder Foundation, a nonprofit organization that is dedicated to the enhancement of human life through research and education on the relationship between the mind, the body, and the spirit. The mission of the foundation is to integrate medicine and spirituality to provide hope, inspiration, and healing to those who suffer from emotional and psychological barriers to personal fulfillment.

Other books by Michael R. Binder, M.D.

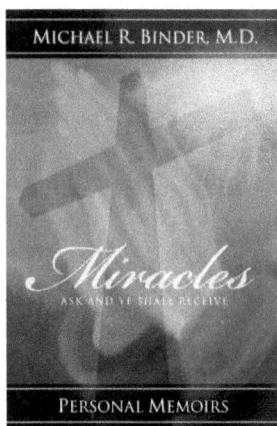

Miracles: Ask and Ye Shall Receive

Miracles is a book of personal memoirs that recounts the acts of God in the life of Dr. Michael Binder, a physician and scientist, who has witnessed the loving hand of God through faith time and again. Packed with more than one hundred miracles, this inspirational work describes the experiences of the doctor himself, which are presented with the historical accuracy and detail that one would expect from a clinical scientist. Those who believe in God will be strengthened by this book; those who are uncertain will be inspired; and those who do not believe will be challenged to take the leap of faith that opens the door to heaven on earth. Available at www.barnesandnoble.com and www.amazon.com

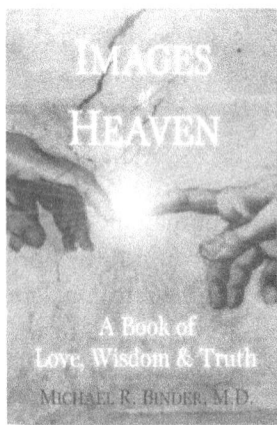

Images of Heaven: A Book of Love, Wisdom & Truth

This unique work is a study of the Holy Bible through the lens of science. Based on the most authentic complete Bible manuscripts in existence, Dr. Michael Binder combines his medical training and experience as a psychiatrist with the knowledge and insights of world-renown Bible scholar Dr. George M. Lamsa to help you understand the entire Bible, from the book of Genesis to the book of Revelation, in the language of our modern culture and times.

Images of Heaven is available only through The Binder Foundation. To learn more or to place an order, go to www.binderfoundation.com.

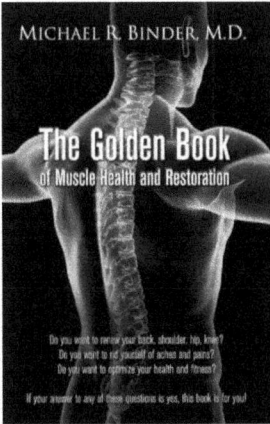

The Golden Book of Muscle Health and Restoration

The Golden Book is a revolutionary look at the hidden cause of chronic musculoskeletal pain and the only effective way to treat it.

Based on his own struggles with chronic pain and the brilliant work of Dr. Thomas Griner, Dr. Michael Binder addresses the little-known but extremely common problem of *hypertonic muscle spasm*. In this life-changing book, you will discover how hypertonic spasm develops, how it causes symptoms, and if you are already suffering from it's ill effects, what to do to get out of pain and stay out of pain without the need of drugs, injections, or surgery. We're talking about truths that are destined to revolutionize orthopedic medicine, physical rehabilitation, and the fitness world! So if you want to preserve the vitality of your muscles and get the most out of them; or, conversely, if you have ever thrown out your back, developed chronic pain in a joint, or experienced frightening symptoms like numbness, tingling, or pain down an arm or leg, this book is for you! Available at www.barnesandnoble.com and www.amazon.com